HAUNTED
TALLADEGA COUNTY

KIM JOHNSTON AND SHANE BUSBY

Published by Haunted America

A Division of The History Press

Charleston, SC 29403

www.historypress.net

First published 2015

Manufactured in the United States

ISBN 978.1.62619.621.6

Library of Congress Control Number: 2015943858

DEDICATED TO THE SPIRITS OF THE DEAD

WHO HAVE REACHED ACROSS THE VEIL

AND INSPIRED US TO TELL THEIR TALES

CONTENTS

CONTENTS

ACKNOWLEDGEMENTS

First of all, we would like to thank the authors who came before us who were so passionate about the history of Talladega County that they wrote their knowledge down and shared it with the world. Without the works of such people as Randolph F. Blackford and E. Grace Jemison, much of the history of Talladega County would have surely been lost. We can't count the number of times that we were speaking with someone and one of these earlier works was quoted. It is our sincerest hope that we can stoke the embers they left behind and ignite a fire of curiosity and hunger for the history of Talladega County in new generations.

Next, we would like to thank all the friends and relatives who stood behind and encouraged us. Writing a book means numerous days spent on research trips and even more long nights of writing. This book would never have been completed if those people weren't willing to sacrifice the time they would normally spend with us. They did so because they knew what this book meant to us, even if sometimes they did so begrudgingly. For that, we thank each and every one of you.

We can't acknowledge the people of Talladega County enough. This book is for you and about you, and we hope that it is something you are proud of. Everyone we met on our journey was so helpful and willing to share their knowledge. Judge Billy Atkinson is one of those people whose time and stories were invaluable to us as we worked on this book. Minister Becky Davis, a true southern lady, was one of the first people we met when kicking off this project. Her support and love of a good ghost story were much appreciated as well. Randy Caine, Mike Waldrop and Stephanie Tipton deserve much praise for bravely sharing their stories with us too. Jessica Bryant, Adrienne Adams and the Green family have all gone above and beyond in their efforts to help us document the stories of this great region. It warms our hearts to know a place with such good people still exists in this world. As our book will show you, bad things happen even in Talladega County, but the people who live there always pull together, pick themselves up and move forward. That's why Talladega County has had such a rich past and why it will also have a rich future.

Last but not least, we would like to thank those who have gone to the other side before us. We will always make sure someone knows your story and you will never be forgotten. It won't be long before we see you again, but until then, you'll always be in our thoughts.

INTRODUCTION

The land that is now Talladega County started making history long before Alabama was even a state. The Creek tribes first settled here because of its beauty and considered many parts of Talladega County to be sacred. Early settlers, no doubt, thought the same things when they first laid eyes on the rolling hills and majestic flowing waterways of Talladega County.

The beauty of the county serves well to hide the scars that have been inflicted on it through the hundreds of years that people have lived here. Today, most people have no idea of the pain and bloodshed that bore itself on the places where present-day people live, work and play. Looking at it now, most would not have an inclination to think that the present-day city of Talladega was a bustling border town serving as a last stop for settlers heading west or that the sleepy town of Childersburg was a center for illegal gambling, bootlegging and prostitution. However, sometimes the sins of people can't be covered up neatly by Mother Nature. Sometimes those sins leave cuts that time can't heal. For some, the crimes they committed have caused them to be bound to the earth as punishment. For others, the atrocities that were done to them can't be forgiven, and they remain here desperately trying to tell their story to others.

Haunted Talladega County isn't your usual book of ghost stories. It's our belief that the most interesting part of a haunting is the back story of why a location is haunted in the first place. We dug deep into the history of this county to bring you tales of everything from the Native Americans being forcibly removed from their land to wars making huge swipes of death and destruction. Each and every one of these tales of human brutality left a mark that lives on today in the form of unexplained events.

While we can't assure you that every tale we are going to share with you is a verifiable haunting, what we can assure you is that every person and place we have written about is undeniably real. Although some names have been omitted by request for anonymity, every story of a modern-day haunting was told to us by a person just like you—a person of Talladega County.

We hope you enjoy reading this book as much as we enjoyed writing it, and we would encourage you to not stop there. This book is about your home; use it as a guide for exploring the mysteries of Talladega County. The overwhelming majority of the places we have written about are open to the public. For those areas that you have access to, go see for yourself whether you believe our stories. If you don't find a ghost, you may very well find your new favorite spot.

Now it's time for our journey to begin. Find yourself a dark, candlelit spot and join us as we paint a picture of the shadowy side of Talladega County.

PART I
CHILDERSBURG

GLORIA'S BRIDGE

It has often been said that every bridge in Alabama is haunted. While Alabama does have a rich history and with that often comes hauntings, it is unperceivable that every bridge in Alabama has a spirit making nightly appearances. However, bridges, like crossroads, seem to be a haven for tragedy and human cruelty. A few of them have more than their fair share of dark stories to tell. One of those is Gloria's bridge.

Gloria's bridge is located right outside Childersburg. Childersburg is one of those towns that reminds you of an unruly teenager who settles downs nicely in old age. It's well known that Phenix City was considered the "sin city" of the South, but in its heyday, Childersburg wasn't far behind. When the United States government announced a contract for a huge ammunition plant—the "shell plant," as old-timers call it—Childersburg's population jumped from five hundred to eighteen thousand in just a couple months. When all those people came, they brought their vices with them. Bootlegging ran rampant, prostitutes set up brothels in rented trailers and there was even a steamboat that harbored an illegal gambling operation tied up on the shore of the Coosa River. All of this put Childersburg on the radar of Governor Frank Dixon. Dixon ordered public safety officials to monitor Childersburg, and fortunately, that's all that needed to be done. Most of the population growth was from temporary construction workers, and when their jobs were done, they left. Without paying customers, the illicit operations left too. After the temporary labor was gone, the shell plant was staffed by permanent local workers (including co-author Shane's grandfather).

Gloria's bridge off County Road 178. *Authors' collection.*

As for the bridge itself, there has been some contention over where the actual Gloria's bridge is located. Some say it is the old bridge next to the newer bridge on Coleman Bridge Road. All that's left of it are the footings, which still protrude from the water. Others say it is the bridge on County Road 178 that is now closed and slowly decaying on gated private property. Given their proximity of only a mile or two and the fact that historical documents can only give us an approximate location, it is nearly impossible to tie all the tragic events that have taken place to one bridge. However, due to the multiple deaths that have been reported at or near these bridges, it wouldn't be surprising if they are both truly haunted. The evidence suggests that Gloria, the well-known ghost that haunts these sites, may not be alone.

The first known incident at Gloria's bridge was in 1885. As a man was walking across the bridge, he spotted a small white pine box in the water. He could plainly see it, as there was only about three feet of water in the creek at that time. He notified the authorities, and upon further investigation, the body of an infant was found inside. The box had been weighted down before being placed in the creek, but apparently, not enough rocks were used, which allowed the box to be washed downstream. It came to rest on a sandbar just below the bridge. The child's demise was blatantly intentional. A small pair of scissors had been stabbed into its left side, and a cord had been wrapped around its neck several times. The citizens of Childersburg were justifiably in an uproar. It happened that the man who found the box had a wife who was a midwife, and many people felt that she and her husband had something to do with the crime—especially since the man found the box so soon after it had been dumped into the creek. To our knowledge, no one was ever convicted of the murder.

This story could explain why people hear a baby crying on this bridge and could be the origin of the many versions of the tale of Gloria. For those

The wooden planks were removed years ago to keep curiosity seekers from crossing the old bridge. *Courtesy of Kat Hobson.*

who haven't heard the tales, one of the stories begins with Gloria and her baby crossing the bridge on foot in high water. Gloria wasn't strong enough to fight the current that was washing over the bridge, and both she and her baby drowned in the creek. Another story states that Gloria was crossing the bridge in a carriage when she had an accident and the carriage plunged into the water. Yet another similar story, probably updated with the times, is that Gloria had a car accident on the bridge, and she and her baby were ejected from the vehicle and drowned in the river. Other variations include tales of Gloria being a jilted bride or unable to marry her true love and throwing herself off the bridge. There's even a variation of this tale that says she died at the bridge on her prom night. No matter the story you've heard, they all state that if you park your car on the bridge at midnight and call out to Gloria three times, you'll hear a baby cry or see the apparition of a woman in a white dress. People who have ventured out late at night to call upon Gloria have also reported seeing something like the shape of a body floating down the creek. One witness to the strange occurrences, who asked to remain anonymous, said that he and his father went to the bridge late one night after running some errands many years ago. They parked the car in the middle of it, turned off the ignition and rolled down the windows. After a few minutes, they began to hear a baby cry. The sound got louder and louder until the father decided to leave quickly out of fright. It's a story that's been told over and over by the residents of Childersburg, but the sad tales do not end here, unfortunately.

In 1892, three men broke into the home of Mr. D.C. Bryant in Childersburg. They beat his wife until she passed out and then did as they pleased to her. In response, as was done in those times, a posse was formed to look for the perpetrators. The identities of the men was not found out until the next evening, when a young girl who cooked for the Bryants confessed to being involved in the crime and gave the names of the three men who had assaulted Mrs. Bryant. Will Carter, Jim Roden and Berry Roden were found a half mile away and taken to the Childersburg jail. The men could not be convicted on the cook's word alone without corroborating evidence, so Mrs. Bryant, lying in a hospital bed and barely able to speak, was asked to identify her assailants, who were brought into the room one by one. She motioned with her hand that she recognized Will Carter, but she did not recall the other two men because she could not see them in the dark of her bedroom on the night of her attack. This was all the townspeople needed, though, to conclude that all three were guilty and to trigger a lynching mob that overpowered deputies and swiftly disappeared into the night with the three accused. With ropes around their necks, gasping for breath, their bodies were riddled with bullets and left hanging from the bridge until the next day when they were found.

Even in more modern times, the bridge cannot seem to escape bearing witness to foul play. Near the bridge on County Road 178 hidden in the forest, there is an emerald blue oasis with water so clear that the bottom of the creek can be seen. In the past, before the land was privately owned and gated, people from Childersburg would gather here to swim and escape the sweltering Alabama summers. They simply call this place the Blue Hole. In 1987, a drunken, senseless murder occurred at the Blue Hole, forever placing a dark cloud over Childersburg's little piece of paradise. Four young men—Dennis Chandler, James Limbaugh, Robert Barnes and William Helton—went out riding in Chandler's car. Stopping at several stores, they made multiple purchases of liquor, which fueled this story's tragic end. Barnes began driving Chandler's car when Chandler became too intoxicated to do so himself. When they stopped at another store, they were chased away because Chandler was knocking things off the shelves. They continued their drunken joyride until Chandler began hitting Barnes. Barnes stopped the car, and the two other men beat Chandler and placed him in the back seat. That's when Limbaugh decided that they had to kill Chandler to keep him from telling anyone about the fight. The four men drove to the Blue Hole. According to court records, William Helton walked away, not wanting to be involved. When he came back, Chandler's lifeless body was in front of the car. Barnes was wiping blood from a knife onto his pants, and Limbaugh was visibly ill—either from consuming too much alcohol or from the horrible, senseless act that had just taken place. The three men dragged Chandler's body through the woods and dumped it in the Blue Hole. Chandler's car was stuck in the mud, so the men walked to Limbaugh's relative's house who lived in a nearby trailer, where they changed clothes and got a ride back into town. Chandler's body was eventually found four miles downstream from the Blue Hole. According to autopsy reports, he had seven broken ribs and a six-inch gash in his neck.

The day we went to see the bridge that's now on private property and next to the Blue Hole, we twice had strange things happen to us. At the bank of the creek, we tried to get a photograph of the entire bridge over the water, but each time the photographer raised the camera and focused in on the perfect picture, a branch from a nearby tree would lower directly into the field of view, obstructing the shot. After this happened several times, to our disbelief, we decided to take a chance on it being Gloria's ghost. We called out to her to stop. Only then were we able to get the shot we wanted of the bridge. Several of us that day felt watched and followed as we walked on foot from the bridge down to the Blue Hole. After our exploration, we trekked back to our cars where we had left them at the bridge. As we stood there sharing stories and talking, it was noticed that brush and branches were being pushed aside at the edge of the woods where we stood, almost as if an invisible person had walked up to our group to join in on the conversation. Perhaps Gloria wanted to weigh in on which bridge is the actual Gloria's bridge. As for now, the answer is just one of the many secrets that she keeps.

WILLIAM COSPER

William Yeldell Cosper was born in 1844 and is a man of note in Childersburg. William didn't attract his fame by being a brave and noble soldier fighting in wars on distant shores, nor did he get famous for being an unscrupulous businessman making deals and earning a fortune. He didn't do anything of the sort. He was just your average Joe trying to lead an average life.

What William didn't know is that some unseen force, maybe even God himself, took issue with him. One night, William and his wife, Martha, were enjoying an evening at home when he was struck by lightning. Being struck by lightning is a bad day for anyone, but William was one of the lucky ones and was nursed back to health by his wife and friends. Either William's near-death experience wasn't warning enough for him to change whatever it was that he was doing to anger God or he simply was not meant to go on living because shortly after his recovery, he was struck by lightning again in 1919. This time, there was no saving him, and he died.

The story of William Cosper doesn't end with his death though. His family went through the usual burial arrangements. They laid him to rest in Childersburg Cemetery and erected a headstone. Later, the headstone was also struck by lightning and destroyed. Probably thinking all of this had to be the worst coincidence in the history of mankind, the family erected another one. It was summarily destroyed by lightning as well. At this point, the family was out of money and could not afford another marker for William— especially since this had gone far beyond coincidence and any others they raised were likely to just be demolished.

William Cosper's story isn't one that would necessarily fit the definition of a haunting, but it is without a doubt paranormal and downright weird. It's so weird, in fact, that it is listed as one of the United States' top one thousand strange stories and has even been featured on the *Ripley's Believe It or Not!* television show. You can still visit William's grave today in the Childersburg Cemetery. It's marked simply with a pile of slightly scorched bricks—the remnants of his last gravestone. However, if you do go, don't stand too close.

DESOTO CAVERNS

Two thousand years ago, sometime between 600 BC and AD 1000, the bones of a Native American family of four adults and a baby were laid to rest inside a majestic, onyx-laden cave. To the Native Americans, this cave was known as *Kymulga*, which translates to "healing all," because they believed it to be an enchanted place with medicinal powers. It was a prehistoric age known as the Woodland Period of North America when people used stone and bone tools, made pottery and began favoring permanent dwellings over the nomadic life. Spears, blowguns and atlatls were still the main weapons in use as bows and arrows were not developed until nearly the end of this era. It was also during this time period that the cultivation of three important crops began: maize, beans and squash.

When Spanish explorer Hernando Desoto arrived in the area in the summer of 1540, the young chief of the Coosa, who was only twenty-six years of age, brought a party of eager native villagers with him to greet the Spaniard. The chief, his head adorned with the most colorful feathers and riding in a cushioned chair resting on the shoulders of his men, extended a warm welcome to Desoto while his fellow natives danced and played melodies on their flutes. Desoto and the chief dined together every night during Desoto's stay in the chief's territory. Being a kindhearted and honest fellow, the chief implored Desoto to choose a region anywhere in his terrain to establish a large Spanish colony. Desoto's men set out on daily explorations of the nearby land in their search for precious metals and a suitable place for the colony. Some people today believe that Desoto may have been taken to

A depiction inside Desoto Caverns of how Native American bodies were laid on platforms after death. *Authors' collection.*

the Kymulga Cave in his pursuit. Desoto contemplated the chief's offer for a time and thought the region to be very beautiful, but the gold and silver he sought eluded him here. He wasn't ready to end his quest just yet, so Desoto graciously declined the great chief's liberal proposal.

Despite the kindness Desoto had been shown during his stay, he was untrusting of the natives and took the chief as a hostage to ensure safe passage through the rest of the territory. The chief's people protested and prepared for war, but their plans were quickly squashed by Desoto's men. Some of the native women whom Desoto and his men thought to be very desirable were shackled in chains and made to carry baggage as slaves for Desoto's expedition. The chief pleaded with Desoto to release a few of them before they departed. Desoto agreed, but the rest of the women, sobbing and afraid, left with Desoto and most likely never saw their families again. The chief of Coosa was held hostage until the fall of 1540, when Desoto reached the village of Talisi near the Tallapoosa River and what is now known as Tallassee, Alabama. Throughout his expedition, Desoto became known for his brutal treatment of the natives. In addition to enslaving them, he mutilated and executed them, often without provocation.

Almost two hundred years later, in 1723, another adventurous man— this time from South Carolina—made history at the Kymulga Cave. I.W. Wright, a trader, left Charleston with ten packhorses full of goods to trade with the natives along his route for furs, deerskins, hickory nut oil and other items he could sell to the white settlers back home. It was a particularly harsh winter that year, and no doubt Wright had heard of the Kymulga Cave and its near-constant temperature of sixty degrees. It was a warm escape from winter's biting chill, so he bedded down for the night inside the dark cavern with only the glow of his campfire to keep him company. During his stay, he made the ghastly mistake of carving his name and the year into a rock. When the local natives discovered what he had done, they were outraged. Kymulga was sacred ground, and Wright had desecrated it with his graffiti. They saw to it that Wright would pay the ultimate price for his mistake. His body was left by the rock he carved as a warning to any other travelers who might think of doing the same.

Decades later, George Stiggins, a half-blooded Creek Indian, wrote a historical narrative of his tribe and described how Wright's bones could still be seen inside the cave in the year 1780. He also spoke of a legend that his tribe had about the cave. Evidently, the place has long captured the imaginations of people because early inhabitants of the area believed that the cave was home to fairies. Although the fairies were never seen, their tracks were said to have been found inside, and it was thought that they lived on the numerous bats and swallows that also called the cave home. Most people associate fairies with tales from Ireland, but many Native American cultures also have stories of the "little people."

Another tale about the cave that comes from the Coosa tribe is about how it once was home to a fierce jaguar that brought terror to the local villagers by stealing their children and dragging them to the cave. The Coosa tribe was never able to kill the animal, and when the Abihka tribe wanted to settle near the Coosas, they agreed that they would capture and extinguish the terrible beast for them. The Abihkas dug a deep pit near the entrance of the cave and then covered it with straw to conceal it. They placed a crying baby nearby to lure the jaguar out of his den. The jaguar fell right into their trap as he was preparing to pounce on the baby. The Abihkas threw their torches into the pit and killed the bloodthirsty animal. The bones of the jaguar were retrieved and made into a powder that the warriors would mix with water and drink for strength and bravery. The Coosas and Abihkas became very good friends after this.

If there ever were fairies or jaguars in Kymulga Cave, they were long gone by the time white settlers moved into Talladega County and the native people were driven away after the Creek Indian War in 1813–14, led by General Andrew Jackson. Jackson's army passed within three miles of the cave on its trip to Horseshoe Bend. Legend states that some of the natives trying to escape being seen or killed by Jackson's men took refuge inside the cavern. After that darkest time of Alabama's history had passed with the awful crescendo that was the Trail of Tears, the cave became a favorite recreation spot for local settlers who would travel by horse and buggy to explore the nooks and crannies by lantern light. Such a dim light could not possibly have revealed the true grandeur of the cavern, but generations of people enjoyed it nonetheless. Some of these folks claimed to have explored the cave for many miles beyond Talladega. There have also been claims that one passage inside the cave actually leads to the Coosa River. More than one hundred years passed with the cave only serving as a local curiosity until another war on Alabama soil brought renewed attention.

During the Civil War, embargoes made it quite impossible for the Confederate army to get gunpowder through normal channels. The Confederacy took over the cave in the 1860s from the man who owned it, Mr. Morris, who has been described as a large slave owner. The bat guano that lined the cavern's floor was rich in calcium nitrate and could be used for the production of gunpowder. Through a mining and filtering process that took several days, the men would extract the calcium nitrate and then convert it into potassium nitrate by mixing in charcoal and ash from their campfires. They would then boil down this mixture until all that was left were the crystals, which were ground up and dried in the sun and could be used as gunpowder. After the war, the cave was turned back over to Mr. Morris, who eventually decided to give the cave to one of his former slaves. It remained in the ownership of African Americans for more than fifty years.

When the time of Prohibition arrived in the 1920s and early 1930s, the cave seemed like a good spot for local moonshiner Pete Willy to hide his distillery. The cave concealed the light and smoke of the fire he needed to brew his whiskey, but there was only one problem: the entrance of the cave during those days was a mound of slippery mud. Willy's hard work would all too often be wasted not only on himself and his love of "sampling" but also on the mound of mud as he struggled to carry the glass jugs out of the cave. After breaking far too many jugs on this hill, Willy decided that maybe he should have the people come to him instead. He strung a few electric lights about the cave, which was the first time electricity was used inside its chambers. Willy also set up a bar and tables so his patrons could play poker. The Cavern Tavern, as it was called, turned into a popular speakeasy in no time and even had a live band playing most nights to entertain the crowd. Drunken guests used the cave's stalactites and stalagmites as target practice and tried to shoot several of them down. It's probably quite fortunate that Willy's venture didn't last too long so that the cave's beautiful formations, which take thousands of years to form, weren't all destroyed. Just six weeks into his illicit operation, revenuers found him out and shut it down. Apparently, there were too many drunken brawls at the cave, and it had earned the name of Bloody Bucket.

Today, nothing is left of Pete Willy's operation or any of the former owners who claimed this cave for so long. The only reminder of the cave's use during the Civil War is a well in the floor of the Cathedral Room that the soldiers dug to use for their mining operation. Present-day visitors to Desoto Caverns are encouraged to throw their loose change into the well. It is all collected and added to a college scholarship fund for lucky high school graduates who work at the cavern during the summer months. It's a tradition that the Mathis family, who own the cave now, started in honor of Ida Mathis, the woman who bought the cave in 1912 and began a legacy for her family.

To put it simply, Ida Mathis was quite an extraordinary woman. She was born in Florence, Alabama, in 1856 or 1857 to Mary and Washington Brandon. Her father was a farmer and undoubtedly influenced her passion for agriculture at an early age. However, Ida wasn't content to stay on and work the family's plantation. She was driven to further her education and in 1874 became one of the first women to ever graduate from college in the state of Alabama, attending Synodical College in her hometown. After graduation, she spent time as a faculty member of a college in Oxford, Alabama. She taught natural science and expression. She gained practical farming experience by buying and managing her own plantation after leaving her teaching job in Oxford. What she learned through this experience and through her education inspired her to start teaching other farmers better practices.

When the cotton states were devastated by the ravages of the boll weevil between 1915 and 1917, Mathis was invited to serve as a member of an agricultural committee of some of the wisest leaders in the industry to help find a solution. She was called to Washington and New York on many occasions to consult with government officials and to advise Wall Street financiers regarding the situation. In 1918, the *Times Picayune* called her the "Economic Moses of the South" for all her efforts to educate farmers of the benefits of crop rotation and crop diversification. She traveled the United States teaching her doctrine of "Safety in Food Crops." Mathis was also invited to speak at a number of conferences in her lifetime. One speech she made in St. Louis to the Farm Mortgage Bankers Association of America (FMBA) was so moving that a copy was sent to President Wilson along with a note of appreciation of Mathis's work in the South to improve economic and social conditions.

Not only was Mathis a successful farmer, educator, lecturer and reformer who gave her knowledge freely to others to help better her nation, but she was also a successful financier, which is what brought her to Childersburg. Mathis was interested in purchasing the Kymulga Cave for its onyx, but she wasn't able to get the mining operation off the ground before cheaper Mexican onyx flooded the market and World War I made it difficult to find workers. While it must have seemed unfortunate to Mathis at the time, this turn of events allowed the cave to be preserved and enjoyed by thousands of visitors for more than one hundred years. It's almost as if this enchanted place is protected, even now, by those Native Americans who thought it to be sacred grounds.

In 1965, the Mathis family leased the cavern to Fred Layton, who had the vision to turn the place into a tourist attraction. Ida Mathis had managed to have a large entrance cut for easy access to the cave before her mining operation ended abruptly. Layton took advantage of this and built steps and walkways. He added proper lighting so that guests could truly appreciate the cave's beauty. He also invited a team of archaeologists from the University of Alabama to excavate a particular mound of dirt inside the cave. It was then that the two-thousand-year-old remains of four adults and a baby from the Woodland Period were discovered; they remained on display for several decades. Within just a couple years of opening to the public, thousands of people were visiting each year. Layton retired after managing the cave for ten years, and it was then was renamed Desoto Caverns. The Mathis family continues to operate the tourist attraction to this day.

Joy Mathis Sorenson, daughter of Desoto Caverns' CEO Allen W. Mathis III, is the fifth generation of the Mathis family to work at the park. Joy grew up in a house on the mountain above the cave with the sounds of children playing and laughing at the park below. She always begged her parents to allow her to take her piano down to the cavern grounds so that she could entertain the tourists for tips. While her parents never allowed it, Joy recalled that they did consent to her having a vendor booth one year at the park's annual Native American festival. After collecting a large number of seashells during a family trip to the beach, she had a revelation as to what she would sell at her festival booth—handmade shell necklaces made out of her own bows and ribbons. On the eve of the festival, her loving father stayed up late

Desoto Caverns' entrance today. *Authors' collection.*

into the night to carefully drill holes in the numerous shells Joy had collected. The next day, five-year-old Joy sold the necklaces for twenty-five cents each. The cute little girl with the shell necklaces was a huge hit with festivalgoers. When buyers handed her paper money and saw her struggle to figure out how much she owed them back, more often than not, they told her to just keep the change. At the end of the day, Joy had made over $300—not too bad for a kindergartner! She was hooked after that and insisted that she have her own booth year after year. It was a wonderful place to spend her childhood that, no doubt, influenced her decision to come back after college and learn the family business.

Not everything about growing up on the mountain above the ancient Native American burial ground was ideal though. From the age of six, Joy describes sensing and even sometimes seeing in her home the spirits of Native Americans who were not pleased. They gave off a very negative energy that really frightened Joy. She was able to describe to her father in great detail what one of the spirits looked like. He then researched the description of the regalia, which turned out to be identical to that of a tribe that once called the land home. Her father never doubted the young child in what she reported to him and always took the opportunity to pray with her whenever an encounter left her upset. This taught Joy the importance and the power of prayer—especially since the spirits seemed to leave her alone for a while afterward. These encounters continued throughout her childhood and into college and ultimately inspired her father to find a way to make peace with the restless spirits.

In response to Joy's upset and the apparent upset of the natives, Allen Mathis flew out members of the various tribes that once inhabited the land. Some came from as far away as the state of Washington to perform a peace ceremony on the grounds in hopes of reconciling the atrocities that happened long ago and any current disputes the spirits may have had with the family living on their land and renaming the cave after a man who treated them brutally. It was during this time that the tribes pleaded with Allen to allow them to rebury the bones of the family that was unearthed in 1965 and had remained on display for the curiosity of the tourists. Allen felt that it was the proper thing to do and allowed the tribe members to select a secret location inside the cave to reinter their ancestors. Only the tribesmen in attendance that day know their exact location now.

Allen took the reconciliation a step further and even invited a member of Martin Luther King's family to the park to pray for peace in a private ceremony to release any grudges former slaves may have held against Mr. Morris, the slave owner who had the land long ago. Perhaps their spirits may have taken issue with how the cave was used during the Civil War as well. After these ceremonies and prayers, Joy still sensed and sometimes saw the spirits, but their energy had lifted. They no longer appeared to her as angry. A noticeable sense of harmony came over the land, and she felt much more at ease.

Very few people know that Mathis family members are actually direct descendants of King Charles I of Spain, who commissioned Desoto to come to America long ago. Allen feels that it is his family's destiny to right the wrongs and to be good stewards of this place that has been sacred to so many people throughout history. He feels strongly that he is fulfilling God's mission with his work at the cavern. Joy's husband, Jarred Sorenson, also feels a deep spiritual connection to the land even though he is not from the area originally.

Jarred grew up in Manhattan and spent time as a producer in Los Angeles before heading to the South with his new bride. After his marriage to Joy, he moved with her to Childersburg to become involved with Desoto Caverns. Jarred, a deeply spiritual man like Joy's father, also feels connected to this land in a special way and had a unique experience shortly after his arrival. Jarred, recently married, in a new place and embarking on a new career, recalled that he had taken a quiet moment to himself to pray on the land for his and Joy's future. During his quiet time of meditation, he had what he could only describe as a vision from God that the cave itself was a sacred place of birth like a womb in the earth and that it was full of life. It was odd to him at first, and he didn't fully understand what he had been shown. Later, he learned that many Native Americans had once called the place *Lun-hamga* and *Nanne-hamga*, which translates to "fathers coming out of a hill," because they believed it to be the place of creation of their forefathers. Jarred was amazed and excited. His vision makes sense to him now and has inspired him and Joy to think of new ways to draw people to the park while holding true to the theme that it's a place of creation—perhaps, in this instance, the creation of new ideas that will keep tourists interested for generations to come.

KYMULGA GRIST MILL

K ymulga Grist Mill is located on County Road 46 in Alpine. It was built in 1864 by a German contractor named G.E. Morris by request of Confederate army captain George H. Forney. Forney died from wounds sustained at the Battle of the Wilderness in Virginia before the mill was completed, but his wife allowed construction to continue. The mill is a water mill, meaning it is powered by a large water wheel turned by the flow of Talladega Creek. The millstones, used for grinding grain, were shipped from France and were received and installed shortly after the naval blockades by Union forces were lifted during the Civil War.

The building itself is a four-story structure, including storage area, grain elevators and shelling and bagging rooms. Directly adjacent to the mill is one of only two nineteenth-century bridges still remaining in Alabama at their original locations. The Kymulga covered bridge once provided access to the Old Georgia Road, which was used as a trade route for Native Americans and early settlers. Today, the Kymulga Grist Mill and Covered Bridge are historic landmarks listed on the National Register of Historical Places and operate as a park and educational facility. What was once the corn room has been converted into a gift shop and visitor center.

The fact that the mill is still in existence today is part miracle and partially because of the hard work and determination of people throughout the years who have fought to save it. During the Civil War, most of the gristmills in the South were burned by raiders from the Union army. Somehow, the Kymulga Grist Mill was never found and escaped destruction. When World War II

Kymulga Grist Mill. *Courtesy of Thomas Francis.*

arrived, the federal government annexed much of the surrounding area for the Alabama Ordnance Works (AOW). The AOW was a munitions plant operated by DuPont during the war to manufacture ammunition and also had a part in manufacturing "heavy water" needed to create the first atomic bomb. When the land was cleared off and the excavation began, numerous

Native American artifacts were unearthed. It was apparent that the site had been a village before the mass exodus in the 1830s, but there was no time to waste in trying to preserve them. It was later said that millions of dollars' worth of artifacts were lost due to the construction and looting that took place afterward.

Because of the construction of the AOW, the mill was slated to be closed until a longtime worker, Albert Burton, wrote a letter to President Roosevelt describing the value the mill had to the community and pleading that it not be closed. President Roosevelt responded by granting the mill a pardon. He also sent Albert an American flag and granted him a special security clearance that allowed him to cross the AOW complex twice a day to get to and from work. World War II brought other problems, however. During this time, the mill became infested by rats. In addition to corn, the mill had a thriving business processing wheat, and the rats developed a taste for the silkscreens used to filter it. Because of the war in the Pacific, the expensive silk imported from China was virtually impossible to get. If the rat problem was not dealt with, it would have surely meant the ruin of many wheat farmers in the area and possibly the mill as well. The owners took action, and with help from the University of Alabama in Birmingham, they acquired a number of large white lab rats. The lab rats were much larger than the mill rats, so they proceeded to chase away their smaller competition. Since the lab rats were accustomed to being fed by humans, they presented no danger to the rare Chinese silks.

While researching this story, we had the honor of speaking with the descendants of Albert Burton, the aforementioned savior of the mill. That's where we uncovered some of the spookier stories surrounding the old mill on Talladega Creek. Albert worked at the mill in the 1930s and 1940s. He spent almost his entire life working in various gristmills around the area until retiring to do light carpentry work. He died in 1955.

One night, after receiving a large amount of grain to process, Albert decided to work late, as he often did during times of high demand. The mill had stopped, so it was perfectly quiet. Albert was working alone in the dimly lit bagging room packaging the grist from that day's milling when he began hearing heavy chains being dragged up and down the stairway. Albert was startled but continued working, all the while hearing the sound of the chains moving up and down the stairs. When a friend came to tell Albert that his wife was concerned he had not made it home yet, he decided it was a good time to pack up and go home. He said he occasionally heard the chains other nights while working late but never discovered an explainable source for

Albert Burton at the Kymulga Grist Mill. *Courtesy of Shirley Green.*

the disturbance. If that wasn't creepy enough, Albert often told his children stories of strange lights dancing up and down the creek in the late night.

An acquaintance of Burton relayed to him that he was once at the covered bridge adjacent to the mill when he saw a woman walking across the bridge.

The woman was unremarkable as near as he could tell, but it happened that she was leading a cow with no head. The woman simply walked to the threshold of the bridge, took a look around, reversed direction and walked back across the bridge. The acquaintance of Burton gave chase, but the woman had already disappeared.

Another tale happened not so far from the gristmill, and Albert Burton had a few encounters with the earth-bound spirit while walking home on those late nights after work. The story goes that there was a lady who lived across the railroad tracks from the mill up on a hill. She greatly enjoyed riding in her horse-pulled carriage on days when the weather was nice. On one fateful day, she prepared her horse and carriage and set off for what should have been a relaxing ride. It wasn't long before catastrophe struck. As she was coming down the embankment from her home, one of the wagon wheels ran into the ditch, causing the carriage to overturn. The woman was thrown clear, and one of the metal stays from her corset pierced her side. The unfortunate woman lost her life that day.

Being aware of the story, Albert always glanced into the ditch as he walked by. On one occasion, after working late into the night, he was passing by and

Kymulga Covered Bridge. *Courtesy of Thomas Francis.*

saw a white figure lying in the ditch. The figure had no defined features and he couldn't be sure what his eyes were seeing, but it unmistakably had the shape of a woman. Albert stood there for some time in the dim light trying to determine just what he was looking at until he saw the headlights of an oncoming truck headed his way. The truck stopped, Albert pointed out the figure to the driver and the two stood there in dismay before they decided it was time to vacate the area. Another night, Albert and his daughter Vera were walking by the same spot when Albert began to shout, "Look, in the ditch! She's in the ditch!" Needless to say, the two scurried past the spot; according to Vera's sister Shirley, the incident that night understandably shook the two of them up quite a bit.

During the course of investigating the claims around the gristmill, we consulted a local paranormal research team, Central Alabama Society for Paranormal Investigation and Research (CASPIR), which had the privilege of investigating the mill and the adjacent covered bridge. The team was unaware of the historical claims we uncovered, but its experiences very much back up some of the stories we were told. On the bridge, the team reported seeing a human figure when it was unoccupied by anyone known to be present that night. Members also recorded a strange mist that formed and quickly moved away on their night vision equipment.

Inside the mill, the team saw a ball of light that seemed to curiously inspect one of the investigators as he was setting up equipment. Their audio recorders were filled with the sounds of footsteps moving up and down the second and third floors, a female sigh, several unexplained bangs and a male voice whispering, all while no one living was present. These types of noises were probably what kept a local man who lived in an old white house near the mill up at night. Relatives of the man told the story of how he slept with a gun under his pillow every night because it constantly sounded to him like someone was either in his house or trying to break in. Every time he would check to make sure he was indeed alone, no explanation could be found, but every night, it seemed there were droves of people at his house with all the noise that the spirits created. Given the history of this site once being a Native American village, it's quite possible they are still around, carrying on their day-to-day activities.

The Kymulga Grist Mill is a rare gem in its beauty and history. Whether you're looking for a scare or just a place to have a picnic with the family, this place has something to offer you. Whenever you're in the area, drop by, stay for a while and let us know if anything strange happens. It is not uncommon for peculiar, ghostly faces to appear in unsuspecting tourists' photos.

PART II

WINTERBORO

WINTERBORO HIGH SCHOOL

Winterboro is located where Highway 76 meets Highway 21. It's a sleepy little town with not a lot of hustle and bustle. However, a little over one hundred years ago, you would have been greeted with an entirely different scene. At that time, it was a hub for stagecoach travel and, thus, was a center of commerce. It provided services to the continuous flow of visitors in and out of town.

In January 1850, the State of Alabama commissioned the Central Plank Road. As the name implies, the Central Plank Road was constructed using planks or pieces of lumber to cover the otherwise dirt roads. The planks served as a smooth surface for the stagecoaches to travel on, providing a much flatter ride than would be had on the typical dirt road and ensuring that the coaches and wagons could run even in times of bad weather when road washouts or heavy mud could strand travelers for days.

At the lead of the Central Plank Road project was a man named Joseph Winter. He originally planned the route for the road to run from Montgomery to Guntersville by way of Talladega. When the people of Talladega unexpectedly pulled their financial support for the project, Winter stopped construction of the road just short of Talladega in present-day Winterboro. He took it upon himself to name the spot after himself.

Winterboro soon began to boom. The surrounding area had plenty of agriculture, but the other roads in the area were little more than footpaths. The only reliable way for the farmers to get their products to market was to go to Winterboro and travel the plank road to Montgomery. The plank road transit system was thought to be cutting edge in its day and was to be the lifeblood of the nation, enabling goods to be transported quickly and dependably throughout the country. The expense and manpower that were needed to maintain the roads became its undoing in the end. The idea of plank roads connecting every major city in the country soon became an unobtainable goal. The plank roads rotted away and, with them, the heyday of the booming town of Winterboro.

The only structure that still stands as a reminder of the old Central Plank Road and the thriving times that it brought is an old home known as the Winterboro Stagecoach Inn. The house is similar to other houses that were built by middle- to upper-class farmers and is known as an I-house. Interestingly, the term "I-house" doesn't refer to the shape of the structure or any particular piece of the building; it is referred to that way because the architecture was popular in states whose names began with the letter I. The Winterboro Stagecoach Inn was built in tandem with the plank road, and for a five-year period between 1850 and 1855, it provided shelter and food to weary travelers and their animals. It was an integral part of the Central Plank Road but outlived it and is now a historical monument to remind people of the era in which it was built.

The school in Winterboro was established around the time of the plank road but has been through various iterations through time. It began its life, like many other schools of the era, as a one-room log cabin. Around 1890, the original log schoolhouse was replaced with a larger two-story structure. Then again, in 1919, the school was replaced with yet a larger building to accommodate the consolidation of several other small schools in the area. The present-day school building was constructed in 1937 and was a community effort, with residents from the area hauling large rocks from a farm and nearby hills to the building site to create the unique stone architecture.

During our research, we've heard several stories from previous faculty and students of the school who report strange happenings. A common occurrence is for the faucets in the bathroom to turn themselves on full blast when no one is occupying the facilities. When people are alone in the building after hours, they have heard their names being called even though no one is there. Also, the doors at either end of the building and the lockers seem to open themselves and slam shut frequently.

The cause of the haunting at Winterboro High School has been a bit of a mystery. While we haven't uncovered any evidence of tragic events occurring on the school grounds themselves, there have been numerous deaths at the intersection of the highway directly in front of the school. In addition, the Winterboro Stagecoach Inn is directly in the vicinity of the school, and we can only imagine the things that happened there and went forever unreported at the epicenter of a wild stagecoach town. It's not uncommon for well-traveled paths of days gone by to seemingly still be in use today by restless spirits. Then again, the haunting could be the result of someone who worked at or attended the beautiful stone schoolhouse in Winterboro and, for whatever reason, decided to spend eternity roaming the halls—perhaps protecting the young men and women who attend the historical learning institution today.

PART III

SYLACAUGA

GRAVITY HILL

Traveling southbound on Highway 280 between Sylacauga and Childersburg, you'll come to a roadside attraction with no signs, no advertisements and no spotlights lighting up the night sky, but if you ask any of the locals, they'll know exactly where it is. If you're the type that doesn't like to ask for directions, it still shouldn't be too hard to find since the road that Gravity Hill is on happens to be aptly named Gravity Hill Road.

While sitting at the stop sign at the intersection of Gravity Hill Road and Highway 280, shift your car into neutral, sit back and be mystified as an unknown force gently pushes you up the incline. It doesn't matter what time of day it is or which way you are facing. Legend has it that a man named Henry was traveling this stretch of road when he had car trouble. Henry got out of his car to push it out of the way and was struck by another motorist and killed. Henry's ghost now faithfully patrols this hill, pushing anyone who has stopped at the top of the hill to keep them from meeting the same fate. This legend is so predominant that some people know the area as Henry's Hill.

Another, less common explanation of the phenomenon is that the road was built over a Native American burial ground. The spirits, not wanting to be disturbed, will push anyone who lingers too long off their resting spot. Those who are more skeptical in nature believe that Gravity Hill is just an optical illusion—it appears you are going uphill when, indeed, you are going down. The cause of this strange, gravity-defying phenomenon may never be known, but if you're ever traveling through Sylacauga and have the urge to have the hair on the back of your neck stand on end, then make a detour to Gravity Hill.

HAMILTON PLACE

Hamilton Place was built in 1854 by Moses Hamilton. It was over three years in the making, with Moses spending endless hours planing the lumber and making every brick by hand to give his bride the home of her dreams. Together, they raised ten children and lived life in a simpler time. Sadly, though, the house was eventually abandoned and spent year after year rotting away while livestock was allowed to trample parts of it, making matters worse.

The Pursell family, realizing what a historic landmark the old home was, decided to restore it to its former glory. To view the old Hamilton Place today is like taking a trip back in time with its elegant mantels over the seven original fireplaces, its original brick floors and its twelve-foot-wide hallways. The Pursells have made Hamilton Place into a guest residence on their renowned country resort so that anyone who desires to experience life in antebellum Alabama is able to do so.

For those looking for more of an adventure, Hamilton Place may possibly hold the key to that as well. Upon speaking with a groundskeeper, we discovered that Hamilton Place is considered by some to be haunted. In addition, he told us that when renovation first began, they found chains and shackles in the old smokehouse behind the home where unruly slaves were sent to be punished. They also found bars over the windows in the basement. This was apparently the slaves' quarters when Mr. Hamilton lived in the home and he wanted to ensure none of them could escape. After touring many homes all over the area similar to this one, this is the first time we've ever encountered shackles and metal bars meant to control slaves. It makes one wonder just what kind of master Mr. Hamilton truly was.

Although they wish to be anonymous, we can say that close family members of one of the authors of this book have spent the night in Hamilton Place. Upon arrival, they were also told by the groundskeeper that the home was haunted but quickly dismissed it as superstition. They put their belongings into a closet in the bedroom and, while doing so, discovered that one of the doors stuck to the old wooden floor in a particular spot and wouldn't move any farther. Nevertheless, they continued to put away their things, locked the closet and locked the exterior doors as they left to drive into town for a late dinner. When they returned from dinner, they were surprised to find the closet doors wide open, and the one door that had caught on the floor before was now pushed all the way open, which would have taken quite a bit of force due to the hump in the floor. Not only were the doors flung open, but the latch on the closet door was now broken and wouldn't remain closed anymore. Much to their displeasure, they had to sleep that night next to the wide-open closet. They had a very uneasy feeling that whatever had flung the doors open did so in protest of their being there. Not much sleep was had that night, and when they returned the following year, they chose to reside in the guesthouse next door, where they slept much better.

BUTTERMILK HILL

Buttermilk Hill is an old Victorian-style home that was built around 1904 and is located in downtown Sylacauga. Its beautiful exterior with an inviting wraparound porch makes you want to pull up a rocking chair and sit a spell on a hot day with a glass of cold iced tea. It is a restaurant today, but for most of its life, it has been a boardinghouse. Not much is known of its beginning days other than that it provided a place for temporary workers to stay overnight and have hot meals. With its five bedrooms upstairs, four bedrooms down and large dining room, there was plenty of room to host guests. It was purchased in 1939 by Homer and Maude Waldrop, who lived in the home for the next thirty-five years and also rented out the extra rooms upstairs.

According to Mike Waldrop, grandson of Homer and Maude, the place was scary and seemed haunted even when he was a child living there in the 1950s. The story of how this place truly became haunted is a sad tale of what his family endured at the hands of his abusive, possibly even demon-possessed father, Joe Waldrop. The stories that Mike has shared in the pages that follow may be hard for some to read, but they are necessary in order to understand just how much pain and negativity this house has harbored—and perhaps still held onto decades later as more tragedy unfolded beneath its metal roof when a senseless murder took place upstairs. The beginning of this home's tragic tale starts with the most beautiful woman in all of Talladega County, Mrs. Violet Waldrop.

Before she married into the Waldrop family, Violet was a straight-A student where she grew up in nearby Harpersville and was a member of her

Buttermilk Hill Restaurant as it stands today. *Authors' collection.*

high school's Beta Club. One night, she attended a dance in Sylacauga at the local community center and met a very charming, dark-haired young man by the name of Joe Waldrop. Soon, the two fell in love and were married. They welcomed their first child, Gary, before Violet could finish school, so Joe decided to enlist in the navy to support his growing family. It wasn't long before they welcomed two more boys, Mike and Jerry, into the world. Joe spent four years in the navy, and when he returned home for good, Violet noticed that he had changed, and not for the better. He was drinking heavily and would have fits of rage.

Joe managed to land a great job working for the railroad, but his alcoholism soon got the better of him. He showed up drunk to work one day and cussed out his boss, who immediately fired him. At home, things were in a downward spiral as well. Joe began locking Violet in their home's closet, where he would leave her for days at a time as he went off on drinking binges. The torture was too much for the sweet young mother to handle. Overwhelmed and traumatized by the ongoing abuse, it was evident that she needed help. She was committed to Bryce Hospital in Tuscaloosa, where she remained for the next six years of her life, recovering from "shellshock," as her son Mike puts it. There was no such thing as post-traumatic stress syndrome back in those days, but today, her family believes this is what she most likely suffered from.

After Violet was committed, it was very clear that Joe was an unfit parent, so the grandparents of the children stepped in to care for them. Violet's parents took the youngest boy, Jerry, who was just an infant. Maude and Homer Waldrop took in Mike and Gary. Violet later recalled that it ripped her heart out to have her family broken up and to lose custody of her babies. Mike and Gary moved into Buttermilk Hill around 1952, and even though their youngest brother did not live with them, the grandparents saw to it that the boys visited every weekend and maintained a close bond.

Life at the boardinghouse with Maude, or "Big Mama," as she liked to be called, was an improvement for the boys. Big Mama was up at four o'clock every morning to cook breakfast and pack lunches for her tenants, most of whom worked for the railroad. The men worked in shifts and shared beds, and the rooms were always packed during the week. Mike remembers helping Big Mama roll out the biscuit dough next to her giant potbelly stove in the kitchen. He and his brother were never allowed to eat in the dining room with the boarders. They sat at a small table in the kitchen tucked away. When midday rolled around, Big Mama was back in the kitchen preparing lunch for the local businessmen in town, who would stop in for her good home-cooked meals. After lunch, she had just enough time to give a few piano lessons to neighborhood children before it was time to start preparing dinner for the hungry tenants who would file in after a hard day's work. One of her piano students, Jim Nabors, who lived next door and was later famous for his role as Gomer Pyle on *The Andy Griffith Show*, undoubtedly grew his love for music in Big Mama's living room under her tender guidance.

It has been said of Big Mama that she was everyone's grandma. She looked after and cared for many of the neighborhood children. She and her husband hosted annual Easter egg hunts for them. Big Mama was a very religious woman and was strict about who she would rent rooms to; if there was any funny business, such as women coming over late at night or any drinking going on, she was quick to address the problem or just throw out the tenant. She instilled her work ethic and love for Jesus into her grandsons, who went to church with her every Sunday. The lessons they learned from her and the faith in God that she nurtured within them would be what gave the boys strength during life's darkest times.

Even though Big Mama was a ray of light in Mike and Gary's lives, they could not escape their evil father, Joe. Often between jobs and quite unstable, Joe would spend the night at Buttermilk Hill at times when he had nowhere else to go. Some of Mike's earliest memories are of his father criticizing Big Mama's cooking in front of the tenants at dinner as a way to

Violet Waldrop with her middle son, Mike, as an infant in front of Buttermilk Hill. *Courtesy of Mike Waldrop.*

embarrass her. He once hurled a plate of food at Big Mama that narrowly missed her head before crashing against the wall. Joe's own father, Homer, was even afraid of him. He slept with a shotgun by his bed and had three locks on their bedroom door. In a drunken rage, Joe even pushed Violet's mother down the front steps of the home when she stopped in to let the youngest brother visit for a while. Several of her ribs were broken. Another time, Mike remembers his granddad having to pull the shotgun on Joe and threaten to kill him in order to stop a violent outburst he was having in front of the boys. Joe left, but it wasn't for long.

Three weeks after the confrontation between Joe and Homer, Joe came by to take the boys for a ride out in the country. Ultimately, it was just a guise for his true, hateful intentions. Joe planned to show the boys who was boss and was still angry that Homer had run him off weeks earlier. He took the boys out into a field, snapped a stick from a tree and commenced to beating Gary across the legs and back, demanding that he say, "You're the boss, Daddy." Gary's will was broken, and he said the words that Joe wanted to hear. Mike, although frightened and upset, wouldn't be intimidated so easily. Joe started beating him too, but through tears and cries of pain, Mike managed to sputter out, "I'm not going to tell you!" Joe continued beating the little boy, but he never relented. After a while, Joe finally stopped and drove the boys back to Big Mama with numerous welts and bruises on their bodies.

As the boys got older and bigger, Joe had to find new ways to torment them, and he especially enjoyed picking on Mike. Joe knew that playing football was everything to Mike in his teenage years. Mike grew up playing with all the neighborhood boys on the lawn of Buttermilk Hill. He played for a couple years on the school's team with all his friends, and then Joe decided there would be no more of it. Mike was crushed. He recalls vividly how alone he felt during this time without his friends and without football. The years of abuse at the hands of his father had taken a toll on him too. He

Joe Waldrop in the 1940s before his addiction to alcohol. *Courtesy of Mike Waldrop.*

started having panic attacks, which he didn't understand at the time. He remembers his heart suddenly racing and feeling overwhelmed. He would run upstairs and hide until his hands stopped shaking.

Though Mike felt alone during these times, his Bible and his best friend, Randy Caine, were always there for him. Randy was also raised by his grandparents and had a drunken father who frequently raised hell. Randy and Mike met in the first grade and were instantly drawn to each other due to their similar home lives. Joe and Randy's father were known to be drinking buddies too at times. Randy remembers seeing his grandfather running both drunken men off from his house one night with a shotgun. Mike and Randy have remained friends to this day; their rocky pasts are a bond between them.

It is quite fortunate that the two friends found each other and had each other to lean on during the worst of times. Big Mama's constant love and support no doubt played a huge role in all of their lives turning out quite all right today. She would often pull Mike aside and speak to him about his father's behavior. Big Mama would tell him that Joe's outbursts should make him never want to touch a drop of liquor. She also confided to him that she believed her son to be possessed by a demon but felt that it was her own fault. She thought that Joe was a curse from God—a punishment for the only lie she ever told in her life.

Evidently, Big Mama, in her younger years, had promised her hand in marriage to another man. When they arrived at the courthouse, she refused to get out of the buggy. She couldn't go through with the wedding because she realized that she truly didn't love him. She broke her promise and asked to be taken back home. For this, she believed God was punishing her by giving her such an evil son. Sadly, Big Mama believed this with all her heart until the day she died.

When the boys graduated from high school, the Waldrops decided to sell the boardinghouse. Mike had lived there for eighteen years of his life, but now it was time for him to stand on his own two feet. It took over a year for the house to be sold. During the time that the house stood vacant, a friend told Mike that he thought someone was breaking into the place because he had seen a man going through one of the windows. Mike decided to check it out one night, and sure enough, he saw a man push open a window and crawl through. He walked over and looked in. He saw a mattress on the floor and realized it was his father, Joe, who had been sneaking in. Mike confronted him, but Joe refused to leave until the place was finally sold.

Homer Waldrop didn't live much longer after selling the place, but Big Mama lived on to the ripe old age of ninety-six. Her final years were spent in a nursing home, and Mike would visit as much as he could. On one of these visits, he arrived and found Joe sitting next to Big Mama's bed, spewing out hateful words just to hurt her. Mike, now a grown man, snapped. He told Joe that he was no longer a scared little ten-year-old boy and he would beat the hell out of his father if he said anything else unkind to Big Mama. Joe sat there silently for the next forty-five minutes until Mike opened the door and motioned for him to leave. Joe didn't come back around the family for several years after Mike stood up to him. He didn't even go to Big Mama's funeral, but he did make a horrible, drunken scene afterward where the grieving family members had gathered. He cursed them all, laughed in their faces and spoke of how much he hated God—something he often said that further convinced Mike that he had a demon possessing him.

When Joe finally died in 1987, only six people attended his funeral, including the minister who was asked to say a few words. Throat and lung cancer had caused him a slow and painful death. Mike dug the grave with his own shovel. He and the family didn't see a need to place a headstone to mark the site. The miserable man met a miserable end, but despite his efforts to ruin the lives of all those he knew, his three boys turned out quite well. All three went to college and have had successful careers. Their mother, Violet, is still alive and well at the age of ninety-six. Mike visits her every week. It would seem that the story of this home and all its tragedy would be over, but sadly, there's one more tale to be told.

After the Waldrops sold the home, it continued to be a boardinghouse off and on. In 1988, newlyweds Stephanie and Chris Allen moved in. Chris was a hardworking man and wonderful father who loved Stephanie's son as his own. Stephanie's mom also lived there in an apartment upstairs. Her mom started dating a new boyfriend who had a sixteen-year-old son, Gary Meeks. It wasn't long before the boyfriend and Gary moved into Buttermilk Hill as well. Stephanie welcomed Gary to the family and treated him like her own brother. Things were great at first. She trusted Gary so much that she even let him babysit her infant son from time to time. Gary was a troubled boy though. Apparently, his home life had not been the best, and Stephanie could overhear him and his father arguing from her downstairs apartment at times. On one of these occasions, it sounded so heated that she ran upstairs and had to intervene. She stood up for Gary, and he said later that no one had ever done that for him before.

The relationship between Chris and Gary also became strained. Although the tension between them was very evident to Stephanie, they would never talk to her about why they were angry with each other. She suspected that Gary may have taken her act of sisterly love, when she intervened in the argument with Gary's dad, the wrong way and perhaps he had romantic feelings toward her. No one except Gary truly knows why he decided to kill Chris, who was just twenty-one years of age. On that horrible day, Stephanie was downstairs tending to her baby boy when she heard a popping sound and Chris cry out in pain from upstairs. She initially thought one of the neighborhood children was playing with firecrackers again and that Chris had just dropped a piece of drywall on his foot since he was renovating one of the apartments for the boardinghouse's owner. Moments later though, several tenants were banging at her door telling her to call 911. She rushed upstairs to find Chris lying on the bathroom floor. He had been shot twice by Gary, who managed to slip out of the house unnoticed. Chris was taken by ambulance to the hospital but later died on the operating room table. Stephanie was devastated. In the weeks prior to his death, Chris had told Stephanie that he would have to leave her soon, even though he didn't want to. Perplexed, Stephanie didn't understand why he would say such a thing. Now, it all made sense—apparently Chris was having premonitions of something terrible happening and was trying to prepare her.

Gary was found in a nearby grocery store hiding between two vending machines. He was sentenced to twenty-four years in prison. Some people believe that a house can harbor negative emotions, as if traumatic events permeate the walls in some mysterious way. Knowing the torment and torture Joe Waldrop put his family through at this home can make a person wonder if that dark energy somehow affected Gary too. After the trial and some time had passed, Stephanie wrote a letter to Gary seeking closure. He confirmed that he and Chris had been arguing that day. He had taken a gun and was planning to use it to steal a car. When the argument broke out, Gary pulled the gun on Chris and fired.

After Chris's death, city officials had the building condemned within a few months. Apparently, the building and some of its tenants had already been deemed a nuisance, so the city was looking for any excuse to shut it down. The home was saved and renovated and then bought and sold a few times after that. In the early 2000s, Kara McClendon purchased the property with her now ex-husband, Nicola Bacchi, with the dream of turning it into a restaurant. Today it is Buttermilk Hill Restaurant and Bar, which pays homage to its past as a place to get good food but also in the name, which originated long ago.

55

As the story goes, there used to be a man who regularly climbed the hill behind the restaurant to buy buttermilk from a dairy on the other side. He would carry the large jar all the way back down the hill, and one day he accidentally dropped it. The local kids playing nearby gathered around, and one of them remarked, "Look at that buttermilk running down the hill!" The place has been known as Buttermilk Hill to locals ever since.

According to Kara and her mother, Algalene, who helps run the restaurant, the place has had some strange happenings over the years. When Kara first moved in, her dog acted quite strangely. Large cans of green beans were inexplicably shoved off the kitchen shelves on more than one occasion. A mist was also seen in the kitchen that formed into a man with black hair before disappearing and frightening all who saw it. The man with black hair has been seen by others too.

Around closing time one evening, a waitress saw a short man in black clothing and long black hair run through the restaurant. The waitress thought it might be Kara for a second and didn't know why she'd be running toward the side door through the dining area. At the same time this apparition was seen, the chimes on the front door jingled. This prompted Kara to come from the bar area to see who was coming in the front door, which she knew was already locked. The waitress and Kara could not explain who the person was or what had just happened. Mike Waldrop firmly believes that it is the ghost of his evil father still causing mischief in the old home. He never wanted to leave when he was alive, and now, in death, he still thinks he belongs there. However, the description of the ghost also matches, to some degree, Chris Allen, who was killed there in 1988. He was known to have long black hair as well and was not very tall in stature. The man with black hair isn't the only mystery at Buttermilk Hill.

One day, Algalene was all alone in the restaurant and went to the restroom. She heard someone knock on the bathroom door, and it startled her quite a bit. When she came out, she confirmed that the doors were all locked and she was indeed there all by herself. Another time, again alone, she was at the front of the restaurant putting Christmas decorations up and heard a woman say as plain as day, "Help me, I've got to get out of here." She looked outside, thinking it was someone out there, but saw no one. She walked around the restaurant to see if someone had come in, but again, she found no one there. She went back to hanging her decorations and heard the woman's voice say the same thing again. The Waldrop family believes that this woman's voice may be one of their family members who fell into a well long ago. The location of the well is now under the kitchen floor where they've also heard the sounds of moaning. Although the relative did not drown in the well and was rescued, they remembered her cries for help being exactly what Algalene heard. Others have had bizarre experiences here too.

The spirit of a little girl has been seen by patrons in the front dining room. She has long Shirley Temple curls and likes to play peek-a-boo with guests. She typically peeks out around the tables and quickly ducks back behind them when she is seen. One patron reported that late one night, he saw a man with white hair and a white shirt on walk out of the kitchen, through the bar and into a wall. Since that incident, they have remodeled, and they found an old doorway inside the wall where the ghostly man was seen walking. When the patron described what this man looked like, the owner, Kara, immediately knew it was Homer Waldrop. She had seen a photo of him when they bought the place and were cleaning out some of the old items that were stored there. The ghost's attire closely matched Mr. Waldrop's usual wardrobe.

In 2010, Kara felt the activity in the restaurant was too much to handle, so she had the place blessed. The spirits have quieted down a good bit since then. The man with the black hair has not been seen since, which could be a good indicator that mean old Joe was the one causing the problems. Today, the only strange thing that seems to happen is Kara's computer likes to turn on in the middle of the night and start playing the music that's usually only on during business hours that provides ambiance for diners enjoying their wonderful food. Since Kara lives upstairs, it always jolts her out of bed when it happens. The song that usually plays is the old 1961 love song by Etta James "At Last." When we asked Chris Allen's former wife, Stephanie, if this song by chance held any significance to her, she was overcome with emotion. She explained that Chris, who she felt was her soul mate, would often repeat the words of the song's main chorus to her ever so sweetly. There's no question in our minds that Chris has sent a message of his undying love to Stephanie through our collaboration and research into the enigma that is Buttermilk Hill.

FORT WILLIAMS

In 1814, Fort Williams was built along the Coosa River by General Andrew Jackson's troops as a supply post. It was a tumultuous time when hostile Creek Indians, also known as Red Sticks, were intent on stopping the influx of whites into their lands. Other tribes of natives such as the Cherokees and National Creeks were persuaded to fight alongside Jackson's men against their common enemy. Fort Williams would support the huge effort to end the Red Stick faction at the Battle of Horseshoe Bend. With approximately three thousand men made up of mostly volunteers from Tennessee under Jackson's command, they departed Fort Williams on March 24, 1814, toward one of the most important battles of the Creek War.

After a three-day march, Jackson's column approached the enemy Creek town of Tohopeka along the arc of the Tallapoosa River. The Red Sticks had prepared to defend the town by building a zigzag log fortification and acted under the guidance of the great warrior Menewa. Jackson's strategy was one that he had used just months before rather successfully at the Battle of Talladega. He planned to surround the village and cut off any routes the Red Sticks may use to retreat. He also ordered his two cannons to fire on the barricade. After two hours of bombardment, very little damage had been done to the barricade and few Red Stick casualties had been caused by Jackson's men's artillery fire. Impatient Cherokee ally warriors grew tired of waiting for the cannons to bring down the barricade, so they swam the Tallapoosa under fire and stole the enemy's canoes. Seeing that this strategy worked rather well, more than two hundred of Jackson's men swam across the river too, captured the town and then set it ablaze. Now that defenders of the town were surrounded, Jackson ordered his men to storm the fortification. John Maass of the Center of Military History describes how the scene unfolded:

> At about 1230, the drums of the 39th Infantry began to beat the long roll to arms. Major Montgomery took the lead with his regiment in the center and the Tennessee volunteers on either flank, the whole looking like a large wedge of troops. Montgomery reached the barricade first, but fell dead with a bullet to the head. In an instant, the entire 39th had mounted the barricade and became embroiled in savage hand-to-hand combat with the Red Sticks, "in the midst of a most tremendous fire." One of the first to make it over the barricade was Ens. (3d Lt.) Sam Houston. Moments after entering the Creek position, Houston received an arrow in his upper thigh, piercing the groin and taking him out of the action.

The Red Sticks fought hard but in the end were no match for the overwhelming number of men who marched on their town that day. Jackson took 350 women and children as prisoners and marched them back to Fort Williams with him and his men. Jackson's wounded and dead soldiers were brought back to the fort as well. Those who did not make it or later died from their wounds were buried nearby at Fort Williams Cemetery. It is the resting place of more than one hundred Tennessee volunteers and Native American allies.

There were others buried at the fort's cemetery as well over the years. In 1832, during the Creek Trail of Tears, three thousand Creeks were held at the fort, which was used as a holding camp before sending the helpless natives out west. Inadequate provisions ensured the deaths of many who entered the fort's gate. Sickness and overcrowded conditions did not make matters any better. For those men, women and children who suffered so greatly and perished, an unmarked mass grave near Fort Williams Cemetery became their final destination.

The fort sat unused and undisturbed for nearly one hundred years, but in 1914, Alabama Power built Lay Dam on the Coosa River, and the water began to rise. The old fort finally surrendered completely to the water in 1928. Some historians say that the cemetery also now lies beneath the water. Others believe that it survived due to its being on higher ground. In 1925, Judge Vandiver sent an open letter to the Birmingham newspaper describing "burial pits arranged in rows" that were still visible at the cemetery site and not under the water. In 1930, an effort to protect the cemetery died in the House of Representatives, and it was never reintroduced.

Despite the disagreement of the cemetery's location, many of the historic headstones sat along the bank of the Coosa near Sylacauga on private property until 2006, when a real estate investor bought the land that contained the old cemetery. The investor had hopes of developing the highly desirable waterfront property into a new community called Riverbend. The graves were considered an eyesore and interfered with development plans. A private company was hired to do a survey with ground-penetrating radar to see if the ground actually contained the bodies of the soldiers. While no human remains were found, it's still quite possible that this place was the original burial site of the brave volunteers.

The survey was done under strict instructions and a small budget. During its limited research, the survey company found that the tombstones were probably placed at the cemetery between 1937 and 1957 during a campaign to mark Jackson's forts along the Coosa. Due to this, the headstones would not have been placed exactly in line with the graves that held the men. It would have only been a best guess as to where the bodies actually laid. Unfortunately, surveyors were not allowed to search anywhere else except directly in the vicinity of the tombstones. The company's final recommendation was for Riverbend's development company to proceed with caution since there were several areas of the land it had not been allowed to scan with its equipment. Had the company been allowed to search a little more, perhaps it would have found the mass grave of Creek Indians or Jackson's men. The tombstones were subsequently removed and placed elsewhere inside the Riverbend community so that the developer could utilize the prized land. Today, high-dollar homes now sit where the grave markers were once located. Even if the cemetery truly is under the water, it seems crass to remove them simply for profit.

Perhaps that is why spirits here seem restless. Locals have long talked about the mysterious fog that rolls in late at night along this area of the river. Some believe it is the spirits of Jackson's men and the natives rising up from Fort Williams Cemetery. If you look long enough, you just might catch a glimpse of one. It's not hard to imagine the sadness they must feel over what has happened to their eternal place of rest. It should be a call to action for those of us who haven't forgotten to preserve the historic places that we can before greed, or even time, is allowed to destroy them.

PART IV
TALLADEGA

TALLADEGA COURTHOUSE

The city of Talladega wasn't always the stereotypical sleepy southern town that it is today. The name Talladega itself translates to "border town." If that conjures up images of the Wild West, then you wouldn't be too far off. You see, Talladega was in fact a border town in its early days. Settlers heading west would often come through Talladega as their last stop before crossing the vast, hostile territory between Alabama and Texas. You could say that Talladega was the last piece of civilization that these travelers would encounter, and there's only one thing that sets civilization apart from complete anarchy: laws and the ability to enforce them. That's why the building of Talladega Courthouse was so crucial to the area's earliest inhabitants, but it would not come easy.

In November 1813, a group of friendly Creek Indians and a handful of settlers were under siege in Talladega at Fort Lashley by a group of hostile Indians known as Red Sticks. Among the friendlies under assault were Chief Chinnabee and his son Selocta. Folklore says that Selocta waited until after dark, placed a hog skin over his body and made his way unnoticed through the Red Sticks' blockade. Once outside the enemy perimeter, he shed his disguise and ran to deliver a message to General Andrew Jackson, who was camped with about two thousand men at Fort Strother on the Coosa River, near where Henry Neely Dam is today. Upon receiving the distress message, Jackson marched his men down to help. Although he was concerned about leaving the wounded behind at the fort unprotected with much of their supplies, he knew that the destruction of Talladega was imminent and action

Talladega County Courthouse as it stands today. *Authors' collection.*

must be taken swiftly. Their march took them past what is now the speedway and Jackson Trace Road. The engagement that happened next would be known as the Battle of Talladega.

On November 9, 1813, Jackson's strategy was to have his soldiers surround the Red Stick warriors in hopes of entrapping them all. However, despite his orders, three companies fled as the Red Sticks fought mightily against them, which caused a gap in Jackson's line of men. Approximately 700 Red Stick warriors escaped due to this, but when the dust settled, Jackson was victorious. Around 300 Red Sticks had been killed, and another 110 were left wounded. The siege at Talladega had ended, which further strengthened the alliance between Jackson and the friendly Creek Indians. It was considered a major win throughout the United States, and Jackson was praised highly.

As word spread about the Battle of Talladega, it attracted more and more settlers to the area. In addition, many of Jackson's men brought their families back to Talladega to settle after the War of 1812 because they thought the area to be so beautiful and abundant in resources. Most of them initially settled in the Talladega Springs area. Even though many settlers were moving in, the area remained Creek territory until the signing of the Treaty of Cussetta in 1832. Provisions of that treaty allotted one of Jackson's most dependable and trusted interpreters, Joseph Bruner, 640 acres of land. This land became the location for most of downtown Talladega. Interestingly, Bruner was an African American, and since they weren't normally allowed to own real estate at that time, Talladega is quite likely the only town in the United States to be owned by a black man in 1832.

Talladega became a county in December 1832, and as a new county, it needed a courthouse. There were opposing views about where the courthouse should be built. Some people wanted the courthouse to be built in Mardisville, and others wanted it where it is today in Talladega. An election was held, and Talladega won by a single vote. Finished in 1838, it is the longest continuously operating courthouse in the state of Alabama.

During the Civil War, much of Talladega was burned when General Croxton and his raiders entered town. As Croxton's men were setting the town ablaze, the fate of the courthouse and most of the Silk Stocking district hung by a thread. The town's judge, J.M. Thornton, rushed to West Street, where Croxton stood and called out to him. Thornton signaled to Croxton the Masonic sign. General Croxton, also a Mason, agreed to speak with Thornton. Although they were on different sides of the war, the sacred pledge of brotherly love they had each taken as Masons transcended whatever political disputes they had that day. Croxton decided to show mercy on the town. Since then, Judge Thornton has been credited with saving Talladega and the courthouse from total destruction.

The courthouse survived many other near misses through the years. In 1912, a tornado hit, causing extensive damage, and in 1925, the courthouse had a major fire. This time, a man named Knox Camp was credited with saving the courthouse. Camp worked inside the courthouse during the day and held a second job across the street after hours. When he saw the blaze, he knocked out a window and began throwing records, as fast as he could, into the vault. Camp managed to save the majority of the county's records with his heroic deeds.

In addition to the damage to the building itself, the courthouse has had its share of human tragedy as well. In earlier times, the use of chewing tobacco was quite prevalent, so the halls of the courthouse were adorned with spittoons along the walls for visitors to use. Seemingly, not everyone had great aim when it came to hitting the spittoon, so there were often puddles of tobacco juice left on the floors nearby. An elderly man who was at the courthouse tending to his business accidentally slipped in one of these puddles and suffered a head wound that ultimately led to his death. Accidents happen, but other times innocent people meet their fates at the hands of jealous rage and pure evil.

The original 1840s' Seth Thomas clock still keeps time at the courthouse despite several near-disasters at the building over the years. *Authors' collection.*

On February 2, 1878, Eliza Truss and Wesley Embry were preparing to spend the rest of their lives together. They were being married that day by the honorable Judge Thornton. After the ceremony, Eliza sat down by the fire as her new husband went to bring around the horse and wagon so they could depart on their honeymoon. During this time, another man who had been seen roaming the halls of the courthouse that day, George Boswell, sat next to Eliza. The two were seen exchanging some whispered words. When Eliza's husband returned for her, she hastily gathered her things and left with him. The bride was mounting the wagon when Boswell approached again and asked her husband if he could have a word with her. Embry agreed to the request, unaware of Boswell's intentions. In the blink of an eye, Boswell threw an arm around the bride's neck and stabbed her nine times before anyone could stop him. Eliza's heart-wrenching screams could be heard across the courthouse square. She stumbled to the sidewalk, collapsed and died within a few minutes. Boswell, with knife still in hand, walked back into Judge Thornton's office and said, "The deed is done; you can lock me up or hang me or whatever. I don't want to live without her." Interestingly, the legal case that followed this tragic event set the precedence for all insanity pleas in the United States. As for George Boswell, he was convicted of murder and sentenced to death. His case was appealed, but before he stood trial a second time, he escaped from the Talladega county jail. Officers searched for him all over the Southeast, but he was never found.

To this day, the maintenance crew at the courthouse reports hearing unknown bumps and bangs in the stairwells. Sometimes, when they are working late into the evening, they can hear the sound of people whispering in the main hallways that run through the first floor of the building. Phantom footsteps have also been heard up and down the halls on a number of occasions, along with doors opening and closing. It has happened so frequently that the crew tries very hard not to work after hours even though it is much easier to get some of the work done with everyone gone. We can only speculate as to who or what these sounds may be. Could it be the ghost of an accidental death at the courthouse or the restless spirit of a woeful bride? Perhaps it's the former employee Camp, whose dedication prevents him from leaving even in death. Hopefully it's not an insane murderer looking for his next victim. We will never know for sure, but what we do know is that the Talladega County Courthouse is truly a marvel with its beautiful architecture and extensive history.

CLAIRMONT SPRINGS

Clairmont Springs is technically located just across the county line in Clay County, but given its rich history, proximity and sentimental fondness to the people of Talladega County, it is only fitting that it should be included in this book. Clairmont Springs was settled long before recorded history. The first Native Americans to live in the area considered it a place of healing due to its many natural springs. The springs themselves are filled with minerals that include white sulfur, black sulfur, magnesia, chalybeate or iron salt, freestone, arsenic and many others. Clairmont Springs is likely the only place in Alabama with such a variety of minerals in its waters. In addition to the springs, there are three small caves on the property and the remains of an old copper mine.

In 1832, the land was relinquished to the United States government by the Creek Indians. After the inhabitants were forcibly removed, the Morgan family squatted on the property. For those unfamiliar with the practice, squatting is the act of living on a property without having a legal deed to do so. Among the Morgan family was John Tyler Morgan, who would later become a senator. In 1841, John Morgan's brother-in-law, William Chilton, bought the property. In 1854, the land once again changed hands when Bill Jenkins bought 540 acres from Chilton and named the property Jenkins's Springs. Then again in 1906, the Guarantee and Trust Company of Atlanta purchased the land, and a railroad was constructed through Jenkins's Springs. It became part of the Atlantic Railroad, which connected Brunswick, Georgia, to Birmingham, Alabama. The Guarantee and Trust

Company had plans to develop the land but failed in its attempts and, in effect, sold the property to a newly formed corporation called the Clairmont Springs Corporation.

The Clairmont Springs Corporation renamed the property Clairmont Springs. The word Clairmont means "clear mountain." In 1909, the corporation built a hotel and several cabins. In 1911, J.W. Jackson purchased the hotel, springs and 520 acres of land. The hotel became popular under the management of the Jacksons, and people from near and far flocked to Clairmont Springs. Some came for the healing power of the water, but many more came for a relaxing vacation at the hotel and to enjoy one of Mrs. Jackson's meals in the dining hall. During World War I, the train would stop at Clairmont Springs for the passengers to disembark and have meals. This added to its popularity, and many of the former passengers, remembering their fine dining experience, returned to stay at the hotel. The hotel remained extremely popular and operated until 1975, when it closed. It sat vacant for a while and, sadly, was destroyed by fire in the 1990s.

There are heaps of lore and legend surrounding Clairmont Springs. Of course, there is the aforementioned healing springs. Then there are the legends of hidden treasures buried on the property. Way back before the land was developed and the original cabin the Morgan family lived in still stood, a woman by the name of Carrie Haralson used to frequent the area. She would spend her days walking and exploring the woods. On one of these occasions, she came upon a suspicious site. There she witnessed a tree carved with an image of a bird and an arrow both pointing in the same direction. Beside the tree was a mound of rocks. She made note of the location, and upon returning from her excursion, she asked around about it, but no one was able to tell her anything more about the curious tree. The carvings remained on her mind, and about a year passed before she had the opportunity to speak with a Native American about the site she had seen. He told her that if she would have counted the rocks in the mound and walked that many steps in the direction that the arrow and bird pointed, she would have found a treasure that had been hidden by his people before they were sent west on the Trail of Tears. It was a common practice for the Native Americans to hide their treasure for fear of the white settlers taking it. They would mark it in similar ways in hopes of one day returning to reclaim it. In this particular case, the man told her that the tribe had been sending men back for many years to make sure the treasure had not been disturbed.

Miss Haralson, as anyone in her situation would, went back to try to find the riches. She still had a good idea of where it was even though it had been over a year since she visited the site. When she arrived, one can only imagine her disappointment upon discovering that lumberjacks had come through to harvest the timber. All the large trees, including the one with the carvings, had been cut down, and the pile of rocks had been scattered.

According to those who have visited in recent years, the old hotel was haunted. Sometimes at midnight, a ghost train can be heard pulling into the station at the once standing hotel. One of the ghosts that is said to have called the hotel home when it was in operation is that of a young girl who could be heard laughing loudly and playing in the halls. Upon inspection, neither she nor any other child who could be making the noises was ever found. She is reportedly the spirit of a six-year-old girl who was killed by a train while playing on the tracks in 1972.

There is also another louder spirit that could be heard stomping about. It's unknown who the spirit is, but we would like to think it is the ghost of a young man who had a macabre yet somewhat humorous take on life and death. He is now buried in the Clairmont Springs Cemetery, and his tombstone, which he inscribed himself, has a chilling message that has inspired many weekend ghost hunters and adventure seekers alike to go and find it. His name is Henry Horn, and the inscription reads:

> *H.L. Horn*
> *1868–1887*
> *Please remember, man, as you pass by.*
> *As you are now, once was I.*
> *As I am now, you must be.*
> *Prepare for death and follow me.*

If you visit Clairmont Springs in the future, pause for a moment and close your eyes. Perhaps you, too, will hear the faint chug and whistle of a long-ago train or a giggle of the little girl who once haunted the hotel. While it isn't the resort it used to be, there is plenty of adventure to be had. Pay a visit to Henry Horn's grave; no need to leave flowers, as a simple nod and a smile should do. Maybe search for a treasure or two, and if you decide to take a bath in the enchanted healing waters, just remember that arsenic is no longer considered to have health-giving properties.

SLEEPING GIANT

While it isn't your typical story of a haunting, the tale of the Sleeping Giant is a valuable piece of folklore and is quite possibly the oldest legend in Talladega County. Therefore, this book would not be complete without it.

Many years ago, before the white man began to settle the area, there was a rich and powerful chief known by the name of Choccolocco. Despite his great wealth, Choccolocco had one possession he valued above all others: his beautiful daughter, Talladega. Talladega was, in every right, a princess. She was the most beautiful maiden in all the land. As she approached adulthood, Chief Choccolocco, like every father before and after, realized he wouldn't be able to keep her to himself forever, so he sent out word that he was searching for a suitable mate for his daughter. Word spread across the realm, and suitors came from near and far to try to win the hand of the beautiful Talladega. Although many tried, no one caught her admiration.

One day, Talladega was at the spring at the foot of a mountain when she heard singing. It was the most beautiful sound she had ever heard, and it brought joy to her heart. The singing got louder and louder until a young warrior burst through the woods and their eyes met. The young warrior's name was Coosa, and Talladega knew that their fates would be intertwined from that day forward. Talladega and Coosa's relationship blossomed into a beautiful love affair, but Coosa was no fitting suitor for the daughter of Chief Choccolocco. He had no possessions and was smaller than the other

The Sleeping Giant mountain is one of the oldest and well-known legends in Talladega County. *Courtesy of John W. Sherman.*

warriors. While this had no effect on Talladega's love for him, it was of great concern to Chief Choccolocco and his council.

About this time, another suitor came into the picture. A well-known and prosperous chief named Cheaha approached Choccolocco and bargained with him for his daughter's hand. Cheaha became Choccolocco's first choice for his daughter, but upon informing her that she would most likely become Cheaha's wife, Talladega was disgusted and told herself that she would never be wed to the ugly old chief.

The fact that he could not marry Talladega was a great weight on the mind of Coosa. He left the village and wandered about the woods along his favorite stream for days. His only thoughts were of his true love. When he returned, he approached the chief and made clear his intentions to marry Talladega. He told the chief that he had been told that he would one day be larger than any other warrior and that he knew the location of valuable minerals stored on unowned lands. He told the chief that he would lead him to the valuables if he would be allowed to marry Talladega. Coosa's promises enticed Chief Choccolocco. The chief said, "If you can bring me proof that what you say is true, you will have my daughter as a wife."

Coosa was inspired by his conversation with the chief. He set out immediately to prove himself. What he didn't know was that Cheaha had overheard the conversation and followed him. Cheaha was determined to stop Coosa and would take any recourse to do so. He sent for one of his medicine men. The medicine man was known to have discovered an herb that would make a man sleep indefinitely and could only be reversed by an antidote that only he knew of. Cheaha and his medicine man waited until the night had set in before they approached Coosa's camp. Upon discovering him lying in his tent asleep, the medicine man administered his devilish concoction. After he informed Cheaha that the medicine had the desired consequence, Cheaha killed the medicine man on the spot so that the antidote would never be found.

Meanwhile, Choccolocco became impatient waiting on the return of Coosa and set about making arrangements to marry his daughter to Cheaha. Talladega couldn't bear the fact that she was to marry Cheaha and couldn't believe that Coosa would abandon her. She ran away into the woods to look for her lost lover and discovered him lying in a deep sleep. She was unable to awaken him though she tried.

The day of the wedding approached, and the bride was nowhere to be found. The people of the tribe searched the woods for her and found her lying by the side of the sleeping Coosa, sobbing and mourning. Cheaha came to her and informed her that Coosa would never awaken from his sleep. Talladega refused to leave Coosa's side. As she was being dragged away, she plunged a dagger into her own heart.

While the medicine kept Coosa asleep, it also allowed him to grow. Over the centuries, he grew to the size of a mountain. Mother Nature took pity on him and covered him with dirt to keep him warm in the winter. She planted trees to shield him from the summer sun. Talladega never left the side of her lover. She was buried next to him and with that became known as the Bride of the Mountain. Legend says that when the need of the people is great, Coosa will awaken from his slumber. He will be taller than any man alive, and with a kiss, he will wake his bride. They will go forth to rule the land of Coosa, vanquishing their enemies and rewarding those who have done good deeds.

ALABAMA INSTITUTE FOR THE DEAF AND BLIND

The Alabama Institute for the Deaf and Blind (AIDB) describes itself as "the world's most comprehensive education, rehabilitation and service program serving individuals of all ages who are deaf, blind, deaf-blind and multidisabled." AIDB now has several campuses throughout the state, but at the beginning, there was one building: Manning Hall. It was built by the Masonic Order to be used as a school for girls. The Masons, having had some financial difficulty, sold it to the Methodist Church, which also used it as a school. In 1858, Dr. Joseph Johnson moved to Talladega and converted Manning Hall into Alabama's first school for deaf students.

Joseph Johnson went to medical school and had intentions to practice medicine, but his brother Seaborn Johnson, who was hearing impaired, inspired Joseph to work with the deaf and blind. In the early 1850s, Joseph took a position with the Georgia Asylum for the Deaf in Cave Springs. In 1858, he corresponded with Governor A.B. Moore and Superintendent of Education William Perry about the possibility of opening a school for the deaf in Alabama. He was encouraged to do so, and talks began about the location of the school. At first, it looked as though Auburn would be the best location for the school, but no suitable facilities could be found there. Joseph Johnson then settled on Talladega and moved into Manning Hall. Seaborn was his first student, and before the end of the first year, the student body had increased to twenty-two.

Unfortunately, the school opened its doors a mere three years before the Civil War. During that era, the school had to close. When the Northern

Manning Hall on the campus of AIDB as it stands today. *Authors' collection.*

troops moved into the area, the people of Talladega were afraid that the Yankees would steal all their valuables, so they put all their gold and silver in bags and hung them inside the giant marble pillars on the front porch of Manning Hall. To the town's dismay, the Union troops made Manning Hall their headquarters. Surely, they thought, their treasures would be discovered. Fortunately, their valuables never were found, and after the Civil War, the townspeople reclaimed their items.

Soon after the war ended, the school resumed operations and thrived. Until this point, the school had only catered to deaf students. Joseph Johnson's brother-in-law, Reuben R. Ashbury, was credited with expanding the outreach to blind students as well after he suffered injury to his sight as a result of being held captive in a prisoner of war camp. According to historical documents, he was "deeply concerned with helping those trapped in perpetual darkness."

Joseph Johnson was a master at navigating the political waters. Along with securing ever more funding for the school, he made many important friends, one of the most interesting of whom was Alexander Graham Bell. Bell visited Johnson many times at Manning Hall, and as a result, the first telephone in Alabama was located there.

When Joseph Johnson died in 1892, his son Joseph Johnson Jr., otherwise known as Hal, was elected president of the school. It was a role that Hal was basically born into. He lived almost his entire life at Manning Hall with the exception of a few short years when he taught at the Kentucky School for the Deaf. He held the position of president until his death in 1913.

F.H. Manning, the namesake of Manning Hall, took up the reins after Hal's death. At that time, the number of students was at an all-time high of 303. Dr. Manning was able to increase that number to over 500. While this seemed like a good thing, there were some drawbacks. The dormitories were overcrowded, and when a flu epidemic struck in 1925, the close quarters provided an easy method of transmission. Most of the students were ill, and all but four of the teachers were incapacitated by the disease. It was up to these four teachers to care for the entire sick population of the school. They were successful to an extent, but by the end of the endemic, 1 teacher and 5 students had perished.

The flu was a hardship for the school, but worse times were ahead. Dr. Manning retired at the age of seventy in 1929, and only four months later, on October 29, 1929, the worst financial crisis to ever hit the United States happened: Black Friday. The stock market plummeted, and with it so did appropriations for the school. There was no money for maintenance, and the teachers and other staff had their salaries cut by up to 20 percent. The students were malnourished and on the verge of starving. During the darkest times of the crisis, the budget to feed the students was set at a meager thirty cents per day.

By this time, Dr. Daniel McNeil was president of the school. While he had no experience with teaching deaf and blind students, he was a true leader and administrator. His vision was for the school to be as self-sufficient as possible. Administrators bought a farm and increased vocational training in agriculture and trades. The farm was able to feed the students through these difficult times. While most of the country starved, they were able to have beef and pork, luxury items during the Great Depression. The students were also able to farm eggs, tomatoes and peaches and had plenty to go around. The farm paid off again during World War II, when the school once again faced budget cuts. Some figures state that the school was able to save over $40,000 by using products raised on its own farm.

The helm of AIDB has passed hands many more times throughout the years, and today the school has gained fame as the best place in the country for hearing and visually impaired students to learn and grow. With over twenty-two thousand students, surely Joseph Johnson would be proud of the legacy he left behind. Actually, left behind may be somewhat inaccurate. It's fairly well known by the faculty and staff who work at or visit Manning Hall on a regular basis that Joseph Johnson hasn't really left his precious school to be attended to by strangers.

When Joseph Johnson lived in Manning Hall, he was well known for smoking a pipe. When the building was empty and being renovated,

This 1935 historical photo of Manning Hall's basement seems to show some type of anomaly. Could it be the spirit of Joseph Johnson? *Courtesy of Library of Congress.*

several people stated that they smelled pipe tobacco being burned in the basement. It is not an uncommon story; renovations of historic places seem to stir the spirits of the past. Sometimes buildings are left unfinished due to paranormal activity when the contractors run away scared, but fortunately, this renovation was completed despite the strange occurrence.

Lynne Hanner, director of institutional advancement at the school, described an unusual event that occurred one Christmas evening. She was the last one in the building, so it was her responsibility to lock up and shut off all the lights. She did so and went to pick up dinner just around the corner. Moments later on her way home, her route took her back by Manning Hall, where she discovered that the lights were on again. She was certain she had turned them off. When she realized that it was the conference room lights, she had no doubt that Joseph Johnson had done it. His portrait hangs in that room, and people say that they can feel Johnson's presence in there, as well as a few other places in the building.

Michael Lynch, an audiologist who works on campus, has also had some interesting experiences. He primarily works in the Gentry Building. As an audiologist, he is particularly aware of strange noises or voices and is quite inquisitive when they seem out of place. He will go to great lengths to track down the source and keeps a detailed journal of those occurrences at Gentry that cannot be explained. On two occasions, Michael has heard distinct "loud whispering conversations," the first of which he and a colleague heard at the same time. Having looked at Michael's journal entries for these occasions, it is evident that he is no amateur. The entries detailed the date and time, the fact that no one else was present inside or out and whether televisions or radios were on at the time. Michael has maintained a journal of the many things he hears on a regular basis for years. The fact that these two incidents stood out as unexplainable to him makes it quite hard to argue otherwise.

If Joseph Johnson still haunts AIDB, we are sure he means no harm. It's our belief that people who were kind in life are also kind in death. In the case of Joseph Johnson, there is no better example of a person with a compassionate heart and altruistic spirit. Certainly, his ghost continues the mission to look after the people he cared so much for when he was alive.

HAUNTED SOUTH STREET

South Street in downtown Talladega is part of the historic Silk Stocking district that is on the National Register of Historic Places. For those not familiar with the term, Silk Stocking districts are where the wealthy upper class once lived long ago. The beautiful old homes in Talladega's historic district range in year built from 1870 to 1915. There are many fine examples of Queen Anne, Classical Revival, Colonial Revival and other late Victorian styles of homes here. With approximately 120 properties within the district listed on the National Register, there are bound to be numerous tales of ghostly encounters that would likely fill volumes of books. The two stories that we chose to share caught our attention due to their proximity to each other on Talladega's South Street, yet they are quite different indeed. The Cofield House is a charming and cozy cottage unlike Swan Hall with its tall Greek Revival columns. One is a story of a Hollywood actress who always dreamed of seeing her name on the marquee, the other of a good man who saved the lives of a family from the beyond. Surely we've only scratched the surface with these two tales, but we hope you enjoy them nonetheless.

SWAN HALL

Built in 1912, this mansion has also been called the O'Donovan Home and the Browne-Elliot Home. It was built for Judge Cecil Browne and designed by architect Frank Lockwood. The lumber that went into building this home was aged for two years to ensure a long-lasting, high-quality home. No doubt, that is one of the reasons why it still proudly stands today, capturing the imaginations of passersby. Inside, it contains one of only two grand divided, waterfall-style staircases in Talladega. Ceilings are a sweeping twelve feet high, and nine fireplaces are the centerpieces of the home's main rooms. Its stately presence on South Street declares that someone quite important once lived here.

Judge Browne was a well-respected Talladega attorney. He named the home Swan Hall after his ancestors' sixteenth-century home place in Hawkedon, England. He came from a prominent family whose wealth came from owning Montevallo Mines in nearby Shelby County. Browne's father had also served in the Alabama state legislature and was a smart businessman. Judge Browne once remarked that he moved from the Birmingham area to Talladega because Talladega had two railroads and Birmingham had only one. In addition to being an attorney, Browne formed several of the area's corporations, such as the Moretti Marble Quarry. Interestingly, the famous sculptor Giuseppe Moretti once lived in a beautiful house on South Street as well and visited Swan Hall on a regular basis.

On one of these occasions, Moretti brought a famous Italian opera singer with him, and the two performed a musical recital for the Brownes. Moretti sculpted two friezes for the Brownes to hang in their home. Only

The Browne-Elliot House, also known as Swan Hall, as it exists today. *Authors' collection.*

80

one remains today above a parlor fireplace. The other was taken to Florida by one of the home's previous owners when they moved. There were many more interesting guests who visited Swan Hall while the Brownes owned it. A 1928 Democratic presidential candidate, Alfred Smith, visited, as well as 1920s celebrity Lincoln Elsworth, who was the first person to fly a plane to the South Pole.

Judge Browne's wife, Sarah, has been described as an accomplished pianist. They had two children, a son and a daughter, who were raised at Swan Hall. Their son, Rollin, followed in his father's footsteps and became an influential attorney. Their daughter, Nina, was more interested in the arts and loved to paint. Swan Hall was once filled with her murals adorning the walls. Nina wasn't content to stay in Talladega though. She dreamed of being a famous movie star in silent films, so she moved to Hollywood to pursue it.

Although fame eluded Nina, she did have roles in three silent films next to some of the bigger names in the industry at the time. In 1920, going by her married name of Nina Cassavant, she played the role of Genevieve alongside the famous romantic comedy actress Constance Talmadge in *Dangerous Business*. That same year, she landed another small role in the adventure film series *The Phantom Foe* as Esther. The headlining actress in that film was the enviable Juanita Hansen, who, in her prime, earned a whopping $1,500 a week—equivalent to roughly $18,000 a week by today's standards. Sadly, Hansen used part of her earnings on fast cars and cocaine, thus essentially ending her career in the early 1920s. Nina's final appearance on the silver screen came in 1922, when she had a brief role playing the wife of the movie's main character in *The Town that Forgot God*.

After her Hollywood career ended, Nina divorced and remarried Lawrence O'Donovan from New York, to whom she remained married until her death in 1971. After her parents both passed away, the O'Donovans inherited Swan Hall and moved in for a time. Both Lawrence and Nina were active in politics. A 1931 article in the *St. Petersburg Times* announced Nina as head of the National Prohibition Reform group for the state of Alabama, which must have raised a few eyebrows back then—especially considering that Alabama has more than twenty-five dry counties to this day.

In 1982, Bill and Sandra Hurst bought the home and lived there with their three children until 2006. Mr. Hurst owned and operated Buy Wise Pharmacy in town. Just before they moved into Swan Hall, it was being used as apartments and had several tenants. They restored the home to a single-family residence. The home was mostly quiet through the years, but there were some unexplainable things that happened. Their youngest child, daughter Corrie, tells us that the upstairs office always had an uneasy feel to it. Whenever a new friend would come over to see the house for the first time, Corrie would take them to each room for a tour and then ask which room they liked the least. The answer was always "the office." One day her mother, Sandra, was in the office on the telephone while doing some bookkeeping for her husband's store. They kept an old electric adding machine in that room, but Sandra had her back turned to it when something very odd happened. While on the phone, she was perplexed to hear the unmistakable sound of the adding machine printing out data on the paper tape roll even though no one was punching in numbers. It kept going and going all by itself. To add to the confusion, when she inspected the tape, it had printed out symbols and gibberish that did not even exist on the machine's simple keypad.

Sandra wasn't the only one to be startled by odd activity in the home. It wasn't unusual for one of the upstairs televisions to turn itself on and loudly blare static unexpectedly. It startled Corrie's father, Bill, on more than one occasion. Corrie also had her fair share of run-ins with strange occurrences that started while she was in college and still living at home. There were many nights when she had trouble falling asleep due to sounds coming from the foot of her bed where she kept a cedar chest. It often sounded like something was sliding across the chest and falling onto the floor. She would flip on the lights to see what had fallen, only to find nothing out of place. Once, after Corrie returned from a summer trip, the spirit seemed to take things a bit further. As Corrie was unpacking her suitcase, she placed several items, including a stick of deodorant, down on the cedar chest. She took her boots off and placed them on the floor facing the chest. She turned her back to continue unpacking when she heard the sound of something sliding across the chest and dropping into one of her boots. Startled, she almost did not want to look and see what it was. To her surprise, she found the stick of deodorant inside her boot, right side up. There was no logical explanation as to how it got there. If it had just fallen off the cedar chest, it should have landed on the floor or on the toe of her boot. To have landed inside her boot like it did, someone would have had to toss it.

After these experiences, Corrie decided to call a psychic friend for some answers in 2002 as to who this spirit was in her home. Her parents were away on a trip, so she was the only one there. She stepped outside to make the call for fear that her conversation may be overheard by the ghost and cause an upset. Her friend told her that the spirit was a woman and she was unhappy over something that had been taken from the home. When the conversation was over, Corrie went back inside and tucked in for the night. Everything seemed to be fine until she returned to the home after work the following day. When she walked in, she was shocked to find a painting of the home that had hung in the first-floor hallway for as long as she could remember now lying on the table below it. Several ceramic decorative items that had been on display on the tabletop were smashed to pieces on the floor. She inspected the wall and found that the nail that held the painting appeared to have been pulled down forcibly, which left a gash in the wallpaper and plaster. When she turned the painting over, she found an indention in the canvas right on top of where the home's office was located. She got the feeling that the spirit was trying to send her a message, and it rattled her to her bones. Corrie refused to spend the night alone in the mansion and promptly left.

The current owners of the home are Terry and Patty Hill. They purchased the home in 2012 after it had sat vacant and was allowed to deteriorate for some time. Terry dreamed of restoring the mansion but had no idea what he was getting himself into. The home had sustained damage in a storm when numerous large trees had been knocked over, and a faucet had been left running for about a year, which caused quite a bit of damage on the back side of the house. It wasn't the first time in the home's history that it had been abandoned and left to rot. In the 1940s, a fire that started in the detached kitchen in the rear of the home swept up the back of the home, over the top and managed to destroy one of the original columns on the front before it was extinguished. Some of Cecil Browne's charred books still remain in the home's upstairs library as a reminder of this bit of the home's history. After the fire, the home was abandoned until Dr. Elliot bought it and restored it. He has been credited with doing the most to preserve this fine place.

When the Hills moved in, they were told by one of the former owners of a spirit that walked across the home's upstairs floor every night. Each night, the spirit would take the same path through the home and could be heard above the master bedroom. The real estate agent who showed the home to the Hills told them that one prospective buyer was scared off by an apparition of a woman on the grand staircase. Another strange occurrence took place shortly after the Hills moved in. Patty learned that one of her neighbors had married Nina O'Donovan's son, so she was excited to invite the woman over to learn more about the family. When the woman arrived at the front door, she refused to go any farther. She remarked that there was something very unhappy inside the home and quickly left. Patty decided to bless the house and pray for the negative spirit to be gone. Interested in the home's history and the unique character that Nina was, she also created somewhat of a shrine to Nina in one of the main-floor parlors. A beautiful photo of Nina hangs above the fireplace now in this room that shows her standing at the same fireplace long ago. In the photo, the second Moretti piece that was taken from the home can be seen hanging on the wall behind her. The Hills felt compelled to bring the piece back to its rightful home, but unfortunately, a deal could not be reached. Patty feels that perhaps Nina's spirit was the unhappy presence in the home because since she has hung Nina's picture in the parlor, the negative energy has lifted. Perhaps Nina was upset over the missing frieze but is

A portrait of Judge Browne's father, who helped finance the building of this home, hangs in the library above charred books as a reminder of this home's past. *Authors' collection.*

content to see how the Hills have tried their best to bring it back and how they've paid tribute to the home's unique history. Now when Patty's neighbor visits, she says that it feels very happy and peaceful. The Hills couldn't agree more.

THE COFIELD HOUSE

Not far from Swan Hall on historic South Street is a quaint cottage that pales in comparison to some of the grander homes in the area. It was built in 1912 and is known as the Cofield House after the family who lived there the longest. William Cofield was a local car salesman, and his wife, Ferne, was a fashion illustrator who had lived in New York for a time. Ferne's mother also lived with them, according to a 1940 census. Although their home was more humble than the mansions that lined their street, the story of how Mr.

Cofield managed to save the lives of the Massey family from beyond the grave is certainly a tale worthy of being told.

When the Massey family moved into the house in 1978, they were told that Mr. Cofield had died in 1969 in the back room of the home after a lightning strike caused a fire. They didn't think much more of it until some unexplainable things started happening. The first thing that daughter Crystal Massey noticed was the sound of a man coming up from the cellar on stormy nights. The footsteps could be heard going to every window and every door to ensure they were secured tightly. On these nights, the spirit would walk through Crystal's room as well to check on things. Her small dog that slept with her would growl whenever the ghostly man would come through her door. It made them both uneasy at first. Nothing bad seemed to happen though, so Crystal and her little dog grew accustomed to old man Cofield making his rounds. She noticed that her teddy bear also liked to move about the house. She normally left it on her bed but sometimes would find it on the dining room table.

Crystal wasn't the only one who experienced strange things. Crystal's dad also saw and heard things he couldn't explain. One day, when he arrived home, he heard the piano playing as he approached the front door. He also heard a man and a woman singing and having a great time. Being that no one was home except for him, it perplexed him quite a bit. He opened the door, expecting to find strangers sitting at their piano, but found no one in the house at all. Another time, her dad stepped out to the backyard in the

The Cofield House as it exists today. *Authors' collection.*

middle of the hot, steamy summer. He felt a cold breeze and immediately knew that something was not right. He looked up and saw the apparition of a man in a round bowler hat and three-piece suit walk through their yard and then disappear into thin air. This style of hat was popular from the mid-1800s through the first half of the 1900s. It is unknown if the man Massey saw was Mr. Cofield.

The Masseys owned a local frame and gift shop on North Court Street for many years. They often heard a woman's voice eerily calling their names from the dark basement of the store. Encountering the paranormal was not new to them, but nothing could have prepared them for the night that the ghost of Mr. Cofield saved their lives. It was an ordinary evening, but it was warm outside, so Mrs. Massey turned the window unit air conditioner on in their bedroom before tucking in for the night. Her peaceful slumber was abruptly interrupted by someone urgently shaking her by the shoulders. When she opened her eyes, she expected to see her husband standing there, but no one could be seen. Instead, she saw the air conditioning unit had caught fire and their room was quickly filling with smoke. She roused her husband from his sleep so they could put out the fire before it spread. The Masseys believe wholeheartedly that it was Mr. Cofield protecting them and the house—undoubtedly trying to prevent anyone from dying in a fire. The humble car salesman from the small town of Talladega is certainly a hero in our eyes.

TOWN'S END FARM

Town's End Farm is a lovely and immaculately restored farmhouse in the city of Talladega originally built in the 1840s by Dr. James Hendricks and his wife, Sally. Town's End gets its name from the detail that it was, in fact, once at the end of town. Everything needed to build the home was manufactured right there on the property. The bricks for the home were made on site, and the wood was cut down from the very plot the house stands on. It was originally used as a farmhouse and was surrounded by fields as far as the eye could see.

Over the years, Town's End was vacated and began wilting away. It sat that way for decades. In the 1930s and '40s, it was resigned to just being a creepy old house at the end of town. Local teenagers used it as an initiation into various clubs, with the new member having to spend the night in the "Old Haunted House." Finally, in the 1950s, someone saw potential in the home and purchased it.

George Jones and his wife, Alice, fell in love with Town's End and decided to renovate it. George was the grandnephew of Dr. Hendricks, and he wanted to restore the home to its original grandeur. It took them several years of hard work. In order to maintain authenticity, they reclaimed building supplies from a demolished home built in the same time period. Their hard work paid off, and they managed to save the historical treasure that George's ancestors built.

In 1976, Dr. Jimmy and Becky Davis purchased Town's End. If you are lucky enough to ever have the opportunity to visit their home, then you are in

Town's End Farm as it exists today. *Authors' collection.*

for a delight. Aside from the beautiful architecture, the home still boasts many artifacts from the time it was built. In the greenhouse in the backyard, there's a Giuseppe Moretti frieze made of Sylacauga white marble, and a portrait of Dr. Hendricks's wife still hangs above the parlor fireplace. The portrait was painted by Nicola Marschall, who served in the Confederate army as an engineer and is the person who designed the Confederate uniform and the original Confederate flag. Upon learning of Dr. Davis living in the Town's End home, several of his patients commented to him on how creepy the home used to be and how they used to spend the night in it to get a good scare. While speaking with Becky, she laughed at the idea that the house was used in such a manner, as she's never felt anything negative there. However, she has had a few experiences with inhabitants from the past that make her feel her home definitely has the presence of ghosts.

Upstairs, when Becky was coming out of her bedroom one night to check on one of her children, she passed by the top of the staircase and saw someone coming up them. She was startled. She couldn't believe what she was seeing. A boy with blond hair was running up the stairs just like he lived there, but in a split second, he vanished.

The Davises' daughter, Allison, was eleven when she, too, encountered something very odd. One day when she was alone in her bedroom with the windows open, Allison heard horses—bunches of them—galloping by on

Left: A portrait of Dr. Hendricks's wife still hangs in the home today as tribute to the family that built the farmhouse. *Authors' collection.*

Right: The staircase where the apparition of a young boy has been seen. *Authors' collection.*

the road. It was so striking to her that she got up and ran to the window to look out. She didn't see anything out her bedroom window, so she ran to the other bedrooms and looked out. She ran from room to room to peer out the windows, but still she saw nothing. She wasn't frightened but told her mother all about it when she returned home. Out of curiosity, her mother checked to see if it was the day that the rodeo came through town, since horses and riders from the rodeo do normally pass by the house. It was, in fact, not the day of the rodeo. The noises Allison heard could not be explained. There is so much history in the town of Talladega that there's no telling whose phantom horses these were. It could have been the war-hungry Red Sticks galloping to Fort Lashley to overtake it. Or perhaps it was Union soldiers who were known to raid local farms in Talladega for food and supplies. Becky likes to describe it as an "auditory slip" in time, as if, for just a few moments, a portal opened and allowed a scene from days gone by to slip through. It's a most fascinating concept indeed.

IRONATON

When people think about ghost towns, visions of vacant towns built during the gold rush in the Old West usually come to mind. One doesn't typically correlate ghost towns with Alabama, but Ironaton is by all rights a true ghost town right in Talladega County. Ironaton was founded in 1871 by Stephen and Sam Noble and was originally called Clifton. It was the terminus of the Clifton Railroad, which was used to haul iron ore and products from the Clifton Iron Works. It was officially incorporated in 1885 under the name Ironaton.

Ironaton was a bustling town for many decades, driven by the revenue from the blast furnaces and mining operations located there. It had all the major necessities of a small town of that time. There was a jail, fire department, city hall, hotels, four miles of streets and lots of people. Sadly, sometime in the 1930s, the furnaces shut down, and the town of Ironaton slowly died. All that remain today inside the city limits are a few houses.

Before Ironaton was bought by the Nobles, the land was owned by a clergyman named John Seay, who was known as "Uncle John" to the nearby residents. When Uncle John was seven years old, the Native Americans who still lived in the area took quite the liking to him. One day, one of the Native Americans told John that he had something to show him. They walked to a stream, and that is where John was blindfolded and led farther through the woods. Upon reaching their destination, John's blindfold was removed, and he was shown a cave whose walls were lined with silver. After being shown this amazing site, John was blindfolded again and taken home. Shortly thereafter, the Native Americans were forced to leave the area and embark on the Trail of Tears. There was no one left who knew the location of the silver mine. That didn't stop Uncle John from looking for it though. When he was an adult, John became obsessed with the cave and made several attempts to find it again, but his attempts were all in vain. When he sold his land, he used all the proceeds to pay other people to help him find it. He died broke, and to this day, the silver cave has never been found.

People say that before the Native Americans were removed from the area, the tribe's medicine man placed a curse on the land to prevent anyone from finding their treasure. They conjured up hellhounds to protect the land and, more specifically, to guard the cave from those who would steal its treasures. Many still report encounters of these black dogs with red glowing eyes in the nearby area.

That's not all there is to the mysteries of Ironaton though. Oddly enough, there's also a hole. It's about two stories deep and about one hundred feet in diameter, and no one really knows how it got there. Centuries ago, the hole was much deeper, but it has filled in with dirt and debris over the years. The theories about how it came to be are numerous and farfetched. One particularly interesting story is that the hole was caused by a meteor strike. It is true that the area was struck by a meteorite shower in the 1700s, but given the almost perfect one-to-one dimensions of the hole, it is unlikely to be a meteor crater. Some say that the hole was dug by a Spanish explorer who was either uncovering or burying gold treasure. Others say it was dug by Native Americans who were also hiding gold. Still others say that the similarities between this hole and the ones used by the Mayans for human sacrifice are surprising and that the Ironaton hole could have been used for the same purposes. While it is not really known if the Ironaton hole holds the corpses of human sacrifices, it has certainly been known to be a death trap for unwary animals over the years, and local farmers have been known to discard deceased animals in the hole as well. There have been no specific reports of the hole being haunted per se, but given its mysterious nature and seeming hunger for death, there's certainly no reason why it wouldn't be. There are parts of Ironaton that do have ghost stories though.

The old train tracks running through Ironaton have several stories attached to them. One story is that of an old slave named Caleb. Caleb was known to flag down the train on occasion to get an easy ride into town. In fact, it was one of his favorite things to do. He loved it so much that he can be seen alongside the tracks to this day, still trying to flag down a train so he can take a ride.

The other story that we were able to uncover about the old train tracks is of a man known only by the nickname "Cooter Man." Given his name, we can only imagine he was quite the rascal. Well, Cooter had an unfortunate run-in with the sheriff one night, brought on by the fact that Cooter was in the throes of an illicit affair with the sheriff's wife. Cooter was shot and killed by the sheriff on Carlisle Road, which runs adjacent to the train tracks. Cooter's mischief-making didn't die with his physical body though. He still haunts the road that he died on. One of his favorite tricks is to pose as a hitchhiker. When an unsuspecting Good Samaritan stops to pick him up, the story always goes the same way. Cooter never says a word, and as soon as the person giving him a ride looks away, Cooter vanishes into the night without a trace—something he probably wished he could have done when the sheriff found him out!

THE JINX OF TALLADEGA SUPERSPEEDWAY

When most people think of the Talladega Superspeedway, images of brightly colored race cars roaring around the steeply banked track under a clear blue Alabama sky come to mind. Crowds of people descend upon the small towns of Lincoln and Eastaboga in May and October each year to partake in the raucous, and sometimes dangerous, affair that is NASCAR. They wonder if they'll witness the next "Big One," similar to when Bobby Allison's car went airborne in 1987 and a catch fence was all that came between mortal danger and the spectators sitting along the front stretch. Whispers of the Big One are often mixed with talk of the curse of the Talladega track. There are several well-known legends that the track was built on Native American land, but few people actually know about its history as the Anniston Air Force Base or, even before that, when it was the Red Hill plantation—home of Dr. Lewis Archer Boswell, who some claim was the first person to fly a plane.

Dr. Boswell was born in 1834 in Virginia. He has been described as an uncommonly intelligent and versatile man but also terse and impatient. He earned his medical degree from Johns Hopkins University and served as a Confederate surgeon during the Civil War. In 1868, while living in Mississippi, Dr. Boswell began experimenting in aeronautics and built a small model plane. Legend has it that he was ridiculed by locals, who caused him to smash his first model to pieces and throw it into the Yazoo River. His wife said, though, that he was concerned someone would steal his ideas, so he smashed it to prevent this from happening. When he moved to Eastaboga a year later with his wife, Bettie, he began experimenting once more at their plantation, Red Hill.

It is said that with help from one of his farmhands at Red Hill, Dr. Boswell hoisted a plane with a small eight-and-a-half-horsepower engine to the roof of his barn, got inside and had the farmhand push him off. Dr. Boswell claimed that he went airborne, maintained control of the plane and touched down with ease. The farmhand's version of the story says it was more of a glide than actual flying, but Boswell was convinced of his accomplishment of being the first person to fly a plane. During his years experimenting at Red Hill, he was granted a patent for a steering mechanism, as well as a propeller wheel that closely resembled the one that the Wright brothers used during their flight at Kitty Hawk years later. As a matter of fact, Boswell tried to sue the Wright brothers for infringements on his patents. It almost seems as if he had a premonition a decade earlier when he threw his broken model into the Yazoo. Sadly, the court would finally decide against him fifteen years after his death. He went to his grave feeling that the Wright brothers had stolen his ideas and without ever gaining much attention for his contributions to the field of aeronautics. Perhaps Dr. Boswell was the first person to ever feel cursed at this site that is now the Talladega Superspeedway.

In 1942, part of the Red Hill plantation became the Anniston Air Force Base to support the World War II effort and was used as a flying school. It had three concrete runways, a hangar and numerous buildings including a library, classrooms and a social club for officers. It is ironic that the very place where flight, fame and fortune eluded Dr. Boswell became a place where planes took off and landed with ease. It was closed in 1952, seven years after the war ended, and sold to the City of Talladega. It sat unused until the late 1960s, when it was acquired by Bill France and NASCAR. The Alabama International Motor Speedway, as it was initially known, was opened in 1969. The old hangar is still in use today, as well as some of the taxiways and runways, which are used as access roads.

From the beginning, the track was entangled in controversy. Bill France dreamed of building a track longer and faster to rival Daytona International Speedway, but it seemed that dream would turn into a nightmare. At the inaugural Talladega 500 race, drivers protested over safety concerns because there was a problem with tires constantly going flat during practice runs. Tires seemed to only last 8 to 13 miles on the asphalt track when normally they should last at least 100 miles. There was a heated debate between Richard Petty (then president of the now defunct Professional Driver's Association) and France, who insisted that the track was safe. Shortly after this debate, Petty

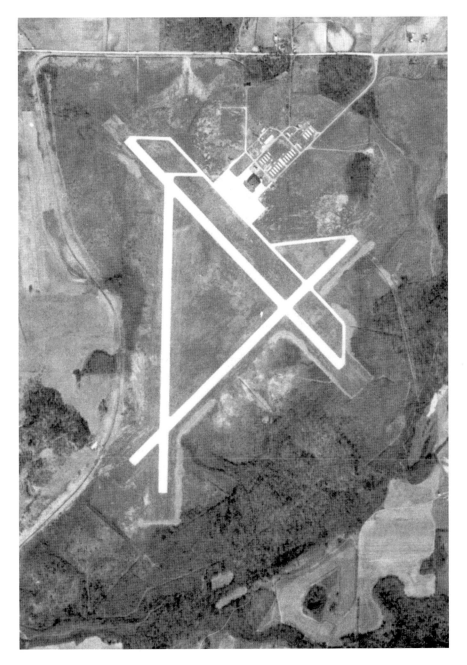

A 1952 aerial photo of the Anniston Air Force Base before the superspeedway was built. *Courtesy of Paul Freeman of www.airfields-freeman.com.*

announced that his organization of drivers would not be racing. It was the first, and so far only, driver strike. To make matters worse for France, Firestone Tire Company announced that it would not supply tires to drivers who would run faster than 180 miles per hour on the new super speedway. France, however, managed to pull off a race without the top-rated drivers with an estimated sixty-four thousand fans in attendance. He pooled together Grand National independents who wanted to race and told them it was "on the house." Newspapers speculated that it cost France anywhere from $250,000 to half a million dollars. Despite its rocky beginnings, the inaugural race kept fans on their feet as three cars, side by side, roared to the finish line. NASCAR driver Richard Brickhouse scored his one and only first-place finish that day.

Tom "Pappy" Higgins of the *Charlotte Observer* was the first reporter to speculate that there may be a curse at Talladega after a strange race weekend in 1996. During that one weekend, driver Bill Elliott broke his leg; Bob Loga, president of the Automobile Racing Club of America (ARCA), was killed in an infield car accident; and driver Ricky Craven went airborne in his car in a pretty serious wreck. Talladega residents told Higgins of a curse placed on the land by the Abihka Tribe of the Creek Indians, who were forced out of Alabama by President Andrew Jackson. Some say that this tribe of Indians held horse races on the land, and a revered chief was killed when he was thrown from his horse. This made the land sacred to his people, so as they were being required to leave, a medicine man placed a curse on the entire valley and anyone who tried to inhabit it. Another legend that is told of this land is that it was an Indian burial ground. Although historians have not found proof of either of these legends, it did not stop Higgins and ESPN writer Ryan McGee from compiling a list of tragedies, bad luck and other strange happenings at Talladega to prove the curse existed.

In 1973, the infamous "Big One" occurred and took out nearly half of the sixty cars racing that day. This is also the same race where Bobby Isaac reportedly heard a voice telling him to "get the hell out" of his car. He pulled off the track and walked away from the race. Later that year at the Talladega 500 in August, Larry Smith, reigning rookie of the year, was killed in what appeared to be a minor single-car crash during a race. His car only sustained a small amount of damage, and his crew was repairing it to return to the race when they received word that Smith was dead on arrival at the infield hospital of head injuries. The following year, someone sabotaged a large number of cars at the Winston 500. Brake lines were found cut, and tires were punctured. The perpetrator even poured bags of sand and sugar into the gas tanks. No one was ever caught.

A present-day aerial photo of the speedway that shows that the old U.S. Air Force base runways and buildings still exist. *Courtesy of Paul Freeman of www.airfields-freeman.com.*

In 1975, there was no celebration at the Talladega 500 after winner Buddy Baker walked off by himself upon learning of fellow driver Tiny Lund's death in the seventh lap. Lund and J.D. McDuffie collided in the backstretch and spun down the track. Rookie Terry Link was also caught up in the crash and slammed right into the driver's door of Lund's Dodge. Link's car burst into flames as two spectators hopped the fence to help. They managed to save Link with help from driver Walter Ballard. However, Lund was pronounced dead at the scene. What makes this story even more tragic is that Lund wasn't even supposed to race in the Talladega 500 that day. He was called in to drive as a last-minute favor when driver Grant Adcox's car was withdrawn from the event. Tragedy also hit the Winston 500 race that same year when Randy Owens, Richard Petty's brother-in-law and crew member, was killed in a freak accident in the pit when a water tank exploded. Owens was only twenty years old and the father of two young boys. It hit Petty and his team really hard to lose Owens. In another freak accident at Talladega in 1977, the mother of journeyman driver David Sisco was killed in the infield when she was struck by the outside mirror of a passing pickup truck. Sadly, this wouldn't be the last fatality at Talladega.

Davey Allison, son of NASCAR racing legend Bobby Allison, considered the Talladega speedway his home track. He was the first second-generation driver in the "Alabama Gang" that was started by his father, his uncle Donnie Allison, Neil Bonnett and Red Farmer. He began his career in 1979 in Birmingham, Alabama, at a short track, where he brought home his first win after only six starts. He was destined to follow in his father's footsteps. During his NASCAR career, he would have 191 starts and win 19 races. His first superspeedway win came at Talladega in 1983 at an ARCA series race. He would go on to win several more times at this track before his untimely death. Undoubtedly, Talladega held a special place in Allison's heart. In 1993, Allison bought a helicopter to transport him to and from races. Three weeks later, he flew it to Talladega with Red Farmer as his passenger to watch David Bonnett during a practice run. The helicopter was a foot from the ground during an attempted landing in a small infield parking lot when it suddenly shot back up in the air. The helicopter began spinning and then plummeted to the ground, landing on Davey's side. Allison was taken to Carraway Methodist Medical Center in Birmingham. He never regained consciousness and died from head injuries. Farmer was treated for a broken collarbone and fractured ribs but survived. Crash investigators at the time did not believe mechanical malfunction of the helicopter was to blame. Tragically, Allison's younger brother, Clifford, had been killed in a single-car crash at Michigan International Raceway less than a year before. The deaths were a huge blow to the Allison family and to the Alabama Gang.

Several years before Davey Allison's death, his father, Bobby, had been involved in a serious wreck at Talladega in 1987 that is also considered part of the curse. His car blew a tire on lap twenty-two in the fourth turn. Speeds were upward of two hundred miles per hour during this race, and his car went airborne. It tore a one-hundred-foot section of the catch fence and injured not only the driver but five spectators as well. Two of them had to be treated at the hospital. Crews needed to repair the catch fence before the race could continue. The race had to end ten laps early due to nightfall and the lack of proper lighting to continue into the darkness. After this wreck, the high-speed, unrestricted races at Talladega came to an end. NASCAR officials made smaller carburetors mandatory and, later, restrictor plates.

In 2009, after Carl Edwards sailed into the front stretch catch fence and flying debris injured seven fans, officials at the Talladega Superspeedway felt that it was time to do something about the curse. Perhaps they, too, couldn't deny that more tragedies and bad luck had happened at their track than anywhere else. On an October day, they invited Creek medicine man Robert Thrower to do a restoration ceremony with the intention of restoring the balance to the land. With a bowl of smoldering tobacco, red cedar, everlasting and wild sage, Thrower offered the fragrant smoke to the four winds and called upon God to protect the drivers. It is uncertain whether the restoration ceremony has ended the long-talked-about jinx. People still whisper these days and now speculate that recent race fan deaths could be a continuation of the curse. The Talladega Superspeedway may never live down its reputation.

TOP TRAILS

Top Trails is the place to go if you want to get muddy. Any given weekend you can see plenty of people splashing around in mud holes on ATVs and even a couple of people on horseback riding the trails that thread in and out of the former army bunkers that are sprinkled in what would otherwise be a large expanse of forest. This area was once a small town filled with neighborhoods and a church. The government bought out the families who lived there in order to build the Coosa Valley Annex, a 2,900-acre property used primarily as a depot for storing ammunition and rations during World War II and the following Cold War. When in operation, it was used mostly by the Anniston Army Depot as overflow storage. The Coosa Valley Annex was slated for closure in 1988 by Congress. It had been inactive for several years, and the closure meant a $100,000 savings for tax payers and required no job cuts.

After the base closure, the land was given to Talladega County with a stipulation that it be used as an outdoor recreation area. Several attempts to do just that tried and all failed until recently, when a group named the Cheaha Trail Riders approached the mayor of Lincoln with their idea to open a park for all-terrain vehicles. Given the fact that federal lands have been closed to off-road vehicles since 1998 and many private landowners prohibit the use of all-terrain vehicles, there was a high demand for such a facility. The cities of Talladega and Lincoln formed an alliance, and with the help of the Cheaha Trail Riders, they were able to raise money through federal grants and selling timber from the property. This allowed them to begin development, and today their work has positioned Top Trails to become a Mecca for outdoor enthusiasts all over the Southeast United States.

While Top Trails is definitely the place to go to get your nature fix, you can also go there to get a dose of hair-raising frights. During the time that Top Trails sat vacant, is was a haven for the teenagers of the area to hang out, build bonfires and play in the mud. As a result, some of the now young adults of the area have some chilling tales to tell about the old army annex. We had the pleasure of meeting Adrienne Adams, one of the aforementioned young adults who frequented the area, who was kind enough to give us a personal tour.

When she was in high school in 2006, she was told a legend that the annex was used for more than just munitions storage: it was also the location for a covert human experiment to try to cross a man with a wolf. The subject of the experiment, a young soldier, died a week later. He left this world unable to find the courage to tell a certain beautiful nurse that he had fallen in love with her. Soon after, people who worked there started seeing a white wolf with human-like baby blue eyes running around the complex. Each time they'd try to catch the wolf, it would vanish.

Adrienne would hang out with friends late into the night at the annex after it was closed down and before it was turned into Top Trails. She never really thought much about the legend until one of her visits when she saw

An old train stop still exists inside the Top Trails park near the site where the mysterious white wolf has been seen. *Authors' collection.*

the white wolf in the distance roaming about just before dark. She tried to point it out to her friends, but each time, it would dart off into the woods before they could see. The second time she saw it, she had wandered away from the group of friends for a few minutes to answer the call of nature, so to speak. As she was sitting there all alone, she felt as if she was being watched. She turned to see a white wolf staring at her. It approached her and sniffed her hair. It stood there for at least five minutes while Adrienne was frozen in fear, unable to move or call for help. When she finally found the courage to try to leave, each move made the wolf snarl and growl. People say that the wolf man is looking for the nurse so he can profess his love, and perhaps he mistook Adrienne for his love. Adrienne did find several different animal skeletons that she could tell were very old behind one of the bunkers one day. A week later, she took a friend back to see them, but they were gone.

At an old church cemetery site on the annex property, Adrienne encountered what could only be described as hellhounds around 8:00 p.m. one night. They appeared skinny and diseased with red glowing eyes. They first circled around her group of friends, snarling viciously. As they all quickly left, the hounds followed her and her friends until they had reached the end of the annex property. These hounds were very different than the white wolf she had seen. They were menacing and definitely evil.

Many of the old munitions bunkers still stand today at the Top Trails park. *Authors' collection.*

Others have reported witnessing strange things at the annex as well. The security guard at the gate check-in said that she has seen an apparition of a Native American while on duty near the entrance where she sits. Other people have reported seeing Bigfoot at the annex.

Frank Lee, who worked at the annex prior to its closing, said that they only had a basic medical facility that didn't seem to be set up for advanced human genetic experimentation, as the legend would have us believe. However, that was forty years after the war, and it would be unlikely that any scientist performing covert experiments would just leave his equipment lying around. Also, Adrienne's very detailed descriptions of the events she witnessed and her ability to take us to exact locations seemed quite convincing. We can't say for sure if there truly is a vicious pack of otherworldly creatures roaming about or a lovesick werewolf looking for his lost love at the old Coosa Valley Annex. We can say that it is now a gem of Talladega County and should be enjoyed by anyone who likes to spend time outdoors. Our advice—come for the nature, stay for the hellhounds, if you dare.

PART V
MUNFORD

BETHLEHEM CHURCH

On McElderry Road in Munford, there sits a quaint little white church and cemetery with tall, weathered tombstones. The church's cheerful red double doors beckon you to visit on a Sunday morning to hear the good word preached from the pulpit. You can almost hear those old-timey hymns being sung when the breeze catches the old branches of the large oak trees that surround this place. It is called Bethlehem Methodist and was built in the early 1800s. It was organized by Judge Tarrant. The actual date the church was built is somewhat elusive, but records show that it had a thriving Sunday school by 1843 with a superintendent, secretary, librarian, teachers and thirty pupils.

The Methodist Church of the time was very progressive. Issues over slavery caused a splintering of the church from other churches during the nineteenth century. Some sects of the Methodist Church were active in freeing slaves through the Underground Railroad, and slavery was officially banned by members in 1816.

The Reverend Joseph Camp, a self-taught minister who moved from Georgia to Alabama in 1833 and who was a friend of Judge Tarrant, was an instrumental figure in the forming of Bethlehem Methodist Church and is even buried in the cemetery adjacent to the church. Reverend Camp's home still stands less than a mile away from the church and is now a bed-and-breakfast known as The Cedars. He and his wife raised twelve children in the home, and Reverend Camp preached in the church as well as at a circuit of churches in the nearby vicinity. From the looks of the beautiful home and

Historic Bethlehem Methodist Church as it stands today. *Authors' collection.*

The home of Reverend Joseph Camp, also known as The Cedars. *Authors' collection.*

church that Reverend Camp helped build, one would think that he led an idyllic life in this small southern town. However, not all was as it seemed.

In 1881, an elderly Reverend Camp was lured away from home by his wife and was told she wanted to see Dr. Peter Bryce in Tuscaloosa about her health. Camp's wife of nearly fifty years knew that he was naïve and would easily believe her. After two days of travel by train and carriage, a weary Camp learned the true intention of the trip was to commit him to Bryce Hospital in Tuscaloosa, a medical facility for the treatment of the mentally ill. By today's standards, the reason for his incarceration is absurd, and even by 1880s standards, it seems a bit of a stretch. Reverend Camp was hospitalized for five months for the treatment of a particularly vicious addiction to tobacco. In his wife's defense, she was most likely legitimately concerned for his health. He had been dealing with his addiction for many decades and had some rather severe side effects on the occasions that he tried to quit. On one such occasion, after three weeks of abstaining from tobacco use, he was riding home from preaching at a distant gathering when he began feeling disoriented to the point that he no longer knew where he was. He had to dismount from his horse to take a break and gather his bearings before he could continue home. Nevertheless, Reverend Camp felt abandoned by his family and was furious about the horrible treatment he received while being detained in the institution.

Upon his release, he wrote a book entitled *An Insight into an Insane Asylum*, which entails the horrors bestowed upon him by the staff and other inmates. Sadly, Reverend Camp was beaten and injected with an unknown drug that caused vivid hallucinations. On his first day at Bryce, he arrived very late in the evening. His wife then explained to him that he would have to stay. He was stripped of all personal belongings and whisked away to a small cell for solitary confinement. The cell lacked any furniture—not even a stool for him to sit on. There was only a mattress on the floor and a box to use as a toilet. He felt terribly betrayed by his family and quite despondent. He wept uncontrollably and later recalled it to be the worst night of his life. There was no one there to reassure him or comfort him or even bring him water when he was overcome with thirst. He called out many times asking for water, but no one came. He begged and prayed for someone to bring him a drink and was, at last, forced to drink his own urine out of desperation.

Once he was finally released from the cell and introduced into regular life inside the walls of Bryce, other patients shared with him how sometimes they would sneak water to desperate patients being held in the cell on their first nights because the nurses would not. One patient even told him of a man who cried out for water while staff played card games nearby and laughed. That patient was found dead the following morning. Sadly, Camp would be deceived by his family and admitted to Bryce two more times after writing his exposé. One of those times, it was documented that he was committed for "religious excitement." Camp's book paints a picture of a man who strongly believed that this excitement was a virtue, not an illness. It is so well written that it's hard to see what his wife and doctors could have seen in him to make them think he was insane. In addition, Camp's book had a clear message: the treatment of patients in the manner that he was treated at Bryce was inhumane and immoral. He pleaded mightily for a change to the laws that governed the institution so that no man or woman would ever have to endure the hardships he did while he was there.

Perhaps the sadness, anger and frustration over the events that took place in Camp's life shortly before his death could be one explanation for the strange things that take place in and around the old Bethlehem Church. To this day, people report that the window shades of the church will raise themselves without anyone else being present on the property. Strange glowing lights have been reported floating above the cemetery. Local folklore says that driving around the cemetery twice at night will trigger the lights to appear.

The strange lights don't seem to be contained to the vicinity of the church though. They have been seen all along McElderry Road and surrounding areas. However, they do seem to be especially active at the church and at the site of an old hotel not far up the road that was used to hold prisoners during the Civil War. The hotel was only used for a few weeks at the end of the war and was mostly burned when the troops withdrew. At this site, the lights are accompanied by the screams of the soldiers who were housed there. Reportedly, the screams are so loud that they can be heard at Camp's former residence, The Cedars. One has to wonder if Camp was truly disturbed, did these screams coming from the old hotel have anything to do with his multiple confinements at Bryce?

We have also heard several firsthand accounts of a woman who haunts the cemetery and church. One group told us they were stared down by this woman standing at the edge of the road across from the cemetery as they passed by in a vehicle. Once they had passed, they looked in the rearview mirror and she was gone. The other account tells us that a man and his brother-in-law, who had heard of the legends beforehand, decided to go ghost hunting at the church one night. They pulled up in front of the church and turned their car lights off and back on. They saw a woman standing

Bethlehem Methodist cemetery, where strange lights and events have been reported. *Authors' collection.*

in the window on the right of the church. They did the same ritual again, turning their lights off and back on again, but this time the woman had disappeared. Could this be the ghost of Mrs. Camp, watching over the church or perhaps looking for her husband?

One of the authors of this book, Kim, even had a firsthand experience at this place. While on a research trip to take photos of the church, she left her husband in the car at the edge of the cemetery by himself while she ventured out to explore. By the time she had returned, he was in a somewhat rattled state. He said that while he was sitting in the car reading, the car's windshield wipers had mysteriously started by themselves. He had not touched anything on or near the car's steering wheel. It had not been raining that day either, so the windshield wipers were not left on by accident. It was a uniquely strange encounter with something, or perhaps someone, quite mischievous that will never be forgotten.

McElderry Plantation

Modern history inundates us with stories of white settlers hell-bent on acquiring land and fortune, taking it from the natives and pushing them from their rightful territory. Many were killed or relocated to areas not even suitable to sustain life. While that is most certainly true, it wasn't always the case. Sometimes, long-lasting friendships were formed between those very people who should be enemies. Occasionally, those friendships last into death, and such is the story of Thomas McElderry and Chinnabee.

Selocta Chinnabee was the son of the renowned Indian chief Old Chinnabee. Selocta had no problem filling the large shoes of his father. In fact, he did so in stride. His first mention in the history books was when he and other friendly Creeks were besieged inside Fort Lashley in Talladega by the hostile Red Stick faction. Selocta, needing to escape the fort to get a message to Andrew Jackson, donned a pigskin and snuck through enemy lines rooting and snorting. He is credited for saving the fort and its inhabitants from complete destruction with his heroic actions.

Selocta fought bravely for the rest of the Creek Indian War and was awarded the rank of brigadier general of the Friendly Creek Warriors. This award was given to him personally by Andrew Jackson. Along with the title, he was also given an American officer's uniform and a silver plated rifle inscribed "To General Chinnabee from Andrew Jackson." He gained notoriety among his own people as well and acquired the name Selocta Fixico. Fixico was a warrior rank that translates to "Heartless One." After the war, Chinnabee went to the nation's capital with other chiefs to protest the Treaty of Indian Springs, which surrendered large tracts of their land to the U.S. government. While he was leaning against a pillar, someone made a derogatory remark about Chinnabee. Overhearing this, President Jackson turned to the man and replied, "That is the bravest man I have ever known."

Thomas McElderry first came to Talladega as a young private of the Tennessee Volunteers. He fought alongside Selocta in the Creek Indian War, during which they became great friends. McElderry rose to the rank of colonel before the end of his career. After he left military service, he returned to Munford and settled down near his old friend Chinnabee. As the saying goes, "friends will be friends," and McElderry was well aware of the superstition among the Creeks that if someone had a dream, it was the obligation of whoever the dream was about to make sure the dream came true. Using this to his advantage, one day McElderry told Chinnabee that he dreamed Chinnabee gave him some of his land. Hesitantly, Chinnabee complied and gave McElderry much of his bottomlands, but Chinnabee was no fool. He waited a couple of days and then told McElderry that he had dreamed that McElderry gave him his favorite white horse. A fair trade was had in the end, and both parties were content.

Chinnabee was known to drink heavily, and while on a trip into Mardisville to buy supplies, he partook in the "fire water" quite liberally. On his way home, his horse ran under a low-hanging tree limb. Chinnabee was

The McElderry Plantation home. *Authors' collection.*

thrown to the ground and sustained injuries that took his life. Chinnabee had many white and Indian friends come to wish him well into his next journey. As is tradition for the Creeks, Chinnabee was buried in the floor of the log cabin he lived in. When the Creeks were removed, Chinnabee's granddaughter asked McElderry to protect the grave. McElderry took his duty to his old friend seriously and is known to have fired his gun more than once on would-be grave robbers looking for treasures rumored to be buried with Chinnabee. As time passed and the old cabin rotted away, Colonel McElderry's son Hugh took it upon himself to pour the concrete slab and erect the monument to Chinnabee that still stands today near the intersection of McElderry Road and Twin Churches Road.

Overlooking the burial monument to Chief Chinnabee, the McElderry Plantation's big house and the family cemetery still remain almost in their original condition thanks to the groundskeepers who maintain the property. The house has been remodeled a few times, but care was always taken to make sure it remained true to the time period in which it was built. Much of the original furniture still resides in the home, and personal possessions from the original family decorate the house as if the McElderrys still lived there. The original deed of purchase from Chief Chinnabee is also on display in the dwelling.

We had the pleasure of speaking with Erin Kirk, who happened to be a previous caretaker's daughter. She spent a portion of her childhood at the plantation exploring the grounds and riding four-wheelers with her family. At first, it was the ideal place for her to grow up, but over time, things changed. The stories she shared with us truly make us think that something isn't quite right with McElderry Plantation.

The thing that Erin said stood out to her as the weirdest phenomenon on the plantation was the bees. She recounted a story of a hot summer day when she and her sisters were lounging by the pool. All of a sudden, a colossal swarm of bees began to gather overhead. The bees, as if being directed by an unseen force, flew into the chimney of the old house. Fearing the house was now overrun with live bees, Erin immediately went to inspect. She discovered that they had all come out the other end of the fireplace inside the house, but they were in a massive pile on the floor—dead. There was a smell of rotting flesh almost immediately, something that you don't usually associate with dead insects, and even though it was summer, one wouldn't suspect that flesh would start rotting so quickly. Less than two weeks after the bee incident, a human face was spotted through the window in the room where the bees had died, and a

Selocta Chinnabee's grave site sits near the McElderry Plantation. *Authors' collection.*

lit candle was found burning even though the house had been vacant for a number of years.

Several other incidents of the like happened during the time that Erin lived on the property. It was a common theme on the plantation for insects and other animals to act weirdly. On our visit to the home, we found a dead cat in the swimming pool, which was not being used due to it being winter. Things like this are not entirely unheard of, but given what we had already been

The McElderry family cemetery, where Thomas McElderry is buried. *Authors' collection.*

told about the happenings around there, it rang some internal alarm bells. It is one thing to see strange sights on a haunted property, but McElderry Plantation seems to go a step further and actually curse the people who live there. Erin reported that the caretaker who came before her was critically injured in an accident involving an ATV, and the owner's wife was stricken with cancer while living in the caretaker's house.

Erin's very own family wasn't exempt from the curse either. Her father was a diehard skeptic. He was the type of man who understood hard work, and the only ghost he believed in was the Father, Son and Holy Ghost. At the young age of forty-four, and having only lived there for eight short months, he was stricken with a debilitating, mysterious illness that put him in a wheelchair. Erin and her family left the property suddenly in December 2003, with fear being the primary reason. Erin's father was a fighter and was able to walk again after months of being in a wheelchair and hours upon hours of physical therapy. He still walks with a limp though today—certainly a reminder of the time he bore the curse of McElderry Plantation and lived to tell the story.

HILL ELEMENTARY SCHOOL

Hill Elementary School is located in Munford off Highway 47. The school closed around 2001, and the building has sat vacant since. The old building with its boarded-up windows has been vandalized and now seems to be a place where local kids go to try to conjure up spirits. The school has a long-told legend that it is haunted by the school's namesake, Ophelia S. Hill. Mrs. Hill was the school's principal for many years, and the legend has it that she was struck by lightning and killed on the front lawn of the school. Her ghost is thought to haunt the grounds, watching out for the students and faculty who worked and studied there.

According to the death certificate, Mrs. Hill, in fact, was not struck by lightning on the lawn of the school. The record indicates that she died at her home in Talladega of heart-related issues in 1954 at the age of sixty-three—just one year after the school was named for her. Although Mrs. Hill did not perish tragically on the school grounds, we did learn that another staff member, a janitor, died while locking up one afternoon after school had dismissed, but that was many decades after Mrs. Hill had already passed away.

Even though the school is vacant now, strange things still happen. Lights have been seen inside the school even though there is no power, and strange, ghostly figures dressed completely in black have been reported walking the grounds. One former student recalled that she was touched by someone one night in the gym while she was attending a fall festival at the school. She had just walked through the door when she felt someone's hand on her.

Above: The abandoned Hill Elementary School as it exists today. *Authors' collection.*

Left: A spray-painted warning on the campus of Hill Elementary. *Authors' collection.*

She turned around to see who it was, only to realize that no one was there. Building contractors have refused to work at the site as well because their power tools stop working for no reason while at the school but begin working again days later after they leave.

We received a firsthand account of a dreadful incident from Amy Reeves, who was a member of the faculty from 1984 to 2000. One day during Amy's first year at the school, she stayed late to paint her office. Every time she walked through the gym, she got the unmistakable feeling that someone was watching her. Being busy with her task, she hadn't realized that everyone had left the building and gone home. On top of that, no one knew she was there. She hurried with her task, feeling watched the whole time, and left as soon as she could. The next day, several kindergarten students came in crying hysterically. They had just found the body of a man on their walk to the school. He had been beaten to the point that his face was unrecognizable. Amy never stayed late again without someone knowing she was there.

While it is entirely possible that Mrs. Hill, the janitor or even the man beaten to death on the trail is haunting the old school building, history explains that there is yet another, more terrifying experience that happened in that area and could possibly be the cause for the haunting of Hill Elementary School. On April 23, 1865, fourteen days after General Lee submitted to defeat and surrendered, officially ending the Civil War, the Union army's General Croxton, with his force of 1,500 men, still marched through the South, determined to destroy anything of military significance that could be found. They had just burned the University of Alabama and were marching through Munford en route to West Point, unaware that the war had ended. News traveled slowly in those days, so neither General Croxton nor his soon-to-be adversary, General B.J. Hill, had received orders to stand down. As Croxton approached, General Hill gathered his men. It was a motley troop of about 150 soldiers made up mostly of boys, old men and deserters. They were known as Hill's Layouts.

Hill's men were badly outnumbered—almost ten to one. However, they bravely stood their ground. On the hill where the school stands, a small detachment led by Lieutenant Lewis E. Parson, who would later become governor of Alabama, placed two small cannons and fired on the Yankees several times. This, of course, brought about a rebuttal from Croxton's men, and a small skirmish that would later come to be known as the Battle of Munford took place. The Confederates were quickly overrun and lost the short-lived battle. In the end, two men died during the skirmish: one Union soldier and one Confederate soldier. The Confederate soldier's name was

Andrew Jackson Buttram, and a monument was erected to honor him in 1912 at the site where he fell. Its location is less than a mile away from where the school stands. The original inscription read:

> *In Memory of*
> *Andrew Jackson Buttram,*
> *Confederate Soldier,*
> *Killed here April 23, 1865*
> *During Croxton's Raid*
> *Erected by Veterans and their descendants*

The Battle of Munford is believed to be the last battle of the Civil War east of the Mississippi and Buttram the last soldier killed. It's alleged that the strong emotions involved with battles in some way imprint themselves on the land in which they were fought, leaving behind residual emotions such as anger, dread and fear. Given the history of the land where Hill Elementary is built, it is no surprise that a legend has been manufactured about its former principal to explain the numerous strange occurrences that have taken place there over the decades. Now that the school is derelict and has become a haven for mischievous curiosity seekers who perform late-night rituals to summon the spirits of the dead, there is no telling what phantoms might be encountered there today.

CEMETERY MOUNTAIN

Imagine yourself on a dirt path in the woods of a secluded mountain, surrounded by thousands of decrepit graves. There are dilapidated buildings from days gone by dotting the landscape. As you make your way through the maze of trees and graves, you can't help but feel that something lurks in the shadows, watching. For some, it would be a terrifying experience bringing forth thoughts right out of a horror movie. For those who find this thought exciting, a trip to Cemetery Mountain in Munford is a must. Unlike a horror movie though, there are no tales of machete-wielding masked men or undead zombies roaming about aimlessly here, waiting for an unwitting human to snack on. But Cemetery Mountain does have its share of spine-tingling tales.

Despite its colorful name and seemingly mandatory proclivity to have more than a few ghost stories about it, Cemetery Mountain's origin was purely utilitarian. The mountain is where the dead from nearby Ironaton were buried. Since Ironaton was primarily a mining town, the land was a valuable asset that needed to be mined, and since digging up dead people would have been considered uncouth, the burial area was consolidated onto one small mountain that was more than likely considered undesirable for mining purposes.

Through the years, the dead haven't been the only ones to call the mountain home. It's said that once, an old man lived alone with his dog on the mountain. The old man was out walking one day when a couple of hunters mistook his dog for a deer. The dog was unfortunately shot and

One of the many cemeteries found on Cemetery Mountain. *Authors' collection.*

killed. The old man, perhaps grieving for his only companion, died shortly after. Some years after the demise of the old man, a group of men were hunting on the mountain. Upon hearing a gunshot, they left their posts to investigate and came upon a wounded black Labrador. While trying to aid the dog, they heard a voice behind them of an old man asking if they had seen his dog. Nodding in the affirmative and turning to point the dog out to its owner, they discovered, to their horror, that the dog was gone. When they turned back to the old man, he, too, had vanished into thin air.

Several others have had very similar experiences while hunting on the mountain. Each time, an old man comes out of nowhere asking about the whereabouts of his lost dog, only to disappear without a trace. Additionally, other black dogs have been seen on top of the mountain, this time without the company of the old hermit. Given Cemetery Mountain's proximity to Ironaton, these black dogs may be the same hellhounds that have been charged with protecting the land and silver mine rumored to be located somewhere in the vicinity of the Ironaton community.

While the old man may have lived by himself on the mountain, others have called the mountain home too. An old barn known as the Murder Barn lies in ruins on top of the mountain. It once belonged to a farmer and his family. The farmer became violently insane and did the only logical thing a violently insane farmer could do: he killed his family. After the deed was done, he retreated to his barn, presumably to clean up and do away with the evidence. What came next was a decisive example of revenge from the other side. A hay hook that was tied to the rafters came loose, seemingly by the doing of ghostly hands. It swung across the barn and caught the farmer under the chin, leaving his lifeless body swinging in the barn for others to uncover the grisly crimes he had committed. Small footprints were found in the dust of the loft around where the hook had been tied, but when they were followed, it was quickly realized that they led nowhere. They say that the footprints matched those of the farmer's wife, but that was impossible because the wife had been dead for over twelve hours. People who pass by the barn today have sometimes seen the body of the farmer still hanging there. While this exact story has never been confirmed, locals do remember that a suicide took place at this site several years ago. The house that once stood here has been demolished now, and only the porch steps remain.

One curious settlement on the mountain that is also now abandoned consists of several old homes and a water wheel. No one really knows why the community was built there, but several theories exist. Some say it was a commune used by occult members; others say it was a small town started by retired carnival workers. Whatever the case, it seems that whoever lived there wanted freedom and to avoid the prying eyes of strangers.

There is also a narrow bridge on the dirt road with a wooden floor and steel trusses on either side. Sometime in the 1960s, a young couple was out joyriding after their prom. They had been drinking heavily and were speeding along the dirt road. The young lady had her head out the window of the car when they came upon the bridge. The driver's reaction time was slowed from the alcohol, and he wasn't able to respond in time. The girl was struck by one of the metal trusses on the bridge and was summarily beheaded. Her head dropped into the creek below and was washed downstream, never to be found. The legend says that if you go there at midnight in the month of May, turn your car completely off and place your keys on the dashboard; you will hear the sound of screams followed by the splashing of a human head hitting the water. While this may sound like just another urban legend, a local firefighter was able to confirm that a young woman was indeed accidentally beheaded on this bridge.

Another tale from Cemetery Mountain is of a book, but not the kind most would want to possess. It's said to be the devil's Bible, and it resides in a church on top of the mountain. Supposedly, the book sits on a pedestal inside the church and is there for the taking. However, would-be thieves have another thing coming. The book becomes heavier and heavier the farther away from the pedestal it is moved to the point that it weighs so much that

The dilapidated barn where a supposed murder took place. *Authors' collection.*

it can no longer be held. If the tale of the devil's Bible is true, it seems that the devil has a no-check-out policy in his library. While this story is very well known, no one today knows exactly where this church is located.

Others have seen green eyes lingering about a foot off the ground along the road running across the mountain. The consensus is that the strange eyes are those of imps. In folklore, imps are the servants to sorcerers and

The Cemetery Mountain bridge where a young woman lost her head. *Authors' collection.*

act as their spies. This does give credence to the feeling of constantly being watched while on the mountain.

To further add mystery to the legends surrounding Cemetery Mountain, there are several graves of people buried here who died in the late 1800s and early 1900s that were inscribed with the same words: "Sisters of Love Chamber." Researching this group has uncovered very little information, but that is to be expected when researching a somewhat secretive organization. People over the years have theorized that there was a resurgence of the occult during this period, and this was likely one of the hundreds of covens that were formed back then. However, what little is actually known about the Sisters of Love Chamber suggests that it was a chapter of the Mosaic Templars of America—not an occult organization or coven. The Mosaic Templars of America was a fraternal organization founded by two former slaves in Arkansas in 1882 to aid others like themselves. The group provided important services such as burial and life insurance for both men and women who maintained their monthly dues. It also provided Vermont marble grave markers like the ones found on Cemetery Mountain inscribed with "Sisters of Love Chamber."

Co-author Shane remembers being told stories of green eyes on Cemetery Mountain by his uncle, which inevitably led to several late-night expeditions to the mountain to find them. While he and his uncle never did find them, Shane still cherishes the memories of the hunt and hopes that you will too.

MUNFORD FOUNDRY

Driving past today, you would never know that the old foundry in Munford began its life as a cotton mill in 1908. Now covered in thick kudzu, only two buildings can be seen from the road. In more recent times, it has been used as a Halloween haunted house attraction, but now it sits abandoned after violence brought the attraction to an abrupt end. The place has the right mix of history and tragedy to conjure up local legends, and there are a few. One legend originates from its earliest days as a cotton mill.

While early cotton mills often advertised employment to women as a means of having an independent and stable income, it was not necessarily a place anyone would choose to work if given another choice. In the summer months, the heat was stifling. The air in cotton mills had to be kept hot and humid to prevent the long threads of cotton from breaking as it was being spun. It was full of cotton dust that the machines produced, causing a condition known as brown lung, as well as eye and skin infections, bronchitis and tuberculosis. The oils used to lubricate the machines were carcinogenic and caused various forms of cancer, also known as "mule spinner" cancer. The machines were so loud that many workers suffered from some degree of deafness. Employees had to work thirteen-hour shifts six days a week with only two weeks off during the summer. There were no lunch breaks, so employees ate a quick bite while they labored away—always well aware that they could be easily replaced if they made too many mistakes or didn't work fast enough. A worker in a cotton mill could expect to earn around two dollars per day for his or her services. In contrast, the same worker could expect to

The Munford Foundry as it exists today. *Authors' collection.*

receive seventy-five cents per day working on a farm, so for many, the pay was enough to keep them toiling away in the harsh conditions. Thousands of people flocked to the mills even though they knew the conditions they faced. To most, it was simply a matter of feeding their families, and they were willing to take the risk to do so. Mill villages were set up around a lot of the larger cotton mills to provide cheap housing for the workers. Conditions in some of these communities were also deplorable. They were generally overcrowded with open sewers. These conditions led to cholera outbreaks in many of the mill village settlements.

In addition to targeting women in their employment ads, many mills employed children whenever they could get them. They could pay them less, and they were generally more compliant workers than adults. The minimum age to employ a child was twelve, but that law was rarely enforced and, for a time, was repealed in the state of Alabama after cotton mills lobbied lawmakers in 1894. Children who were too young by law to work were instructed by the mill owners to say they were twelve if asked by authorities. If a child was obviously too young to be working there, he would be coached to say he was just stopping by to deliver meals to his parents or older siblings. Makeshift schools were constructed but generally were only open for eight weeks a year, which was the minimum required for each child to attend by law. This, of course, was usually fudged as well, and some children may have only attended school a few weeks in their entire lives.

It wasn't until after the Great Depression that child labor in the cotton mills dwindled. This wasn't because the greed of the mill owners lessened or that the sketchy child labor laws were finally being enforced. It wasn't even because the owners decided what they were doing was wrong and somehow suddenly grew compassion. It was because of technology. The newer, more efficient machines created during the Great Depression years needed someone with more skill and, more importantly, of greater height to operate them.

After the golden era of the cotton mill ended, the mill in Munford did as well and closed its doors. The old mill sat vacant until 1944, when the Central Specialties Company of Ypsilanti, Michigan, acquired the property. The Central Specialties Company, at the time, was a division of King Seeley and manufactured tools for mail order, most notable of which was Sears. Central Specialties was looking to open a foundry in the South. After touring several sites in Talladega, John Lonskey rented a taxi to take him to Anniston to see a few more. While riding through Munford, he saw the idle mill and realized its potential. He later joked that he never made it to Anniston that day.

Lonskey worked hard to get his business up and running, but World War II was still raging at this time. There was a restriction on the use of steel, so the foundry had to start small. Production was mostly restricted to wartime manufacturing. When the war ended, manufacturing was shifted to the mail-order goods that were Central Specialties' core business. In 1964, Central Specialties sold all of its patents, tooling and inventory to the Emerson Electric Company and ceased doing business.

There is no way to know for sure how many lives the old foundry has claimed over the years. Whether as a cotton mill or a foundry, it was a dangerous place to work. At least two serious injuries occurred during the time the building was functioning as a foundry, and there were multiple fires. Earlier, when it was a cotton mill, the laws weren't as restrictive on reporting such matters, but given the conditions, there is no doubt that people would have been maimed or possibly even killed on the grounds.

Aside from the general loss of limbs, burning and other occupational hazards that would have occurred, it is documented that at least one coldblooded murder happened at the foundry. Albert Lee Reaves, a sixty-nine-year-old night watchman, was found unconscious one night in 1954. He died the next day from two blows he received to the head. A disgruntled former employee was later found to be guilty of the senseless act. Even today, the old foundry seems to have a lust for blood. While it was operating as a

Halloween haunted house in 2005, four teenagers were brutally shot on the property. Thankfully, all survived and were later released from the hospital.

Today, the vacant foundry building is dilapidated, which probably fuels the local folklore. People believe the main building to be haunted by a little girl who fell into a deep hole on the property that was left over from its cotton mill days. Supposedly, there are several of these deep pits hidden under the kudzu, and there have been many people to go missing from the area who are believed to have fallen into these holes. This legend is probably why it was used as a haunted house attraction by the local Jaycees Group in the early 2000s. One of the workers, Jennifer Shropshire, who helped at the haunted house for several years in a row, had heard of the legend surrounding the place, but she didn't think much of it until she worked there.

The first encounter she had was hearing the giggles of a young girl inside when no one else was around. Her co-workers confirmed that they had heard it too at times. Someone found an old child's ball while cleaning up and set it to the side. They were all surprised to find that the ball moved on its own. This happened as well to their tools while they were working to build the haunted house. Jennifer remembers using a hammer and setting it down for just a minute, and when she turned back around to grab it, it was gone. This happened to their makeup, fog machines and other pieces of equipment.

One evening when Jennifer was working with a few of her friends and everyone else had gone home, they saw something none of them could explain. As they approached the foundry along a path at the back of the building, they saw a ball of light hovering near the ground at the entrance. As they got nearer, the ball of light sped toward them, and as it was just about to run into them, it shot off to the right into the darkness. She and her friends were also pursued by a growling dog inside the building one evening. They could hear the growls and the dog's feet rushing up behind them on the concrete floor, but when they turned around, it was gone. Several patrons also complained of a growling dog inside the maze portion of the Halloween attraction, but no dog was ever found to explain it. Jennifer and her friends were perplexed but not overly frightened by these incidents. However, there is a reason why Jennifer has vowed to never return to the foundry, and it causes her chills to even speak of the event to this day.

After the haunted house was shut down due to the shootings that took place there in 2005, the foundry sat empty. Jennifer thought it would be fun to take her boyfriend out to see the creepy building around dusk and tell him of all the strange things that had happened to her there. They parked their car along the path leading up to the building and didn't venture any farther.

As they stood beside the car, they thought they heard something moving about inside the old structure. Jennifer's boyfriend yelled out toward the building and began to antagonize and provoke the spirits to show themselves. Suddenly, a tall shrouded figure appeared at the doorway. Its eyes were white and glowing, but the rest of its body was a shadowy gray. It stepped out of the building and quickly started down the hill toward them. They hurriedly got into the car and left. As they sped away, Jennifer saw in her rearview mirror that it followed them the whole way down the driveway until they had passed the gate. It is for this reason that she will not even drive past the foundry to this day.

There is a second, smaller building on the property that was used for storage during the foundry's haunted house days. People have found pentagrams and upside-down crosses spray-painted on its walls. If the haunting is not due to the death that took place there long ago, it could most certainly be due to the occult rituals that may have taken place on-site. Unless you're willing to tempt fate, maybe it would be a good idea to steer clear of the old Munford foundry and its bottomless pits, snarling dog and shadowy gray phantom.

CAMP MAC

Camp Mac is located in Munford near the base of Cheaha Mountain, where thousands of children have enjoyed summer camp since 1948, when Mr. E.A. McBride first opened the site. It offers many fun activities for young campers such as horseback riding, water skiing, mini golf, biking and swimming. However, many people do not know that it was actually established during the Great Depression to house the Civilian Conservation Corps (CCC), which was a public work relief program that operated from 1933 to 1942. It was a major part of President Roosevelt's New Deal program and provided work for young men who had trouble finding jobs during the Depression.

The work mostly centered on the development of natural resources on federal and state-owned lands. The men received housing, food, clothing, medical care and a small paycheck of thirty dollars per month; they were required to send twenty-five dollars back to their families at home. Enrollees, as they were called, had to be unmarried, unemployed males between the ages of eighteen and twenty-five. A physical exam or a period of physical conditioning had to be undergone to make sure they were prepared for the hard manual labor that awaited them in the corps.

The CCC set up camps locally in each of the areas it did conservation work in. The camps themselves were made to be temporary in nature. The early camps consisted of army tents, but later on, the use of barracks was widespread. The barracks housed fifty men each and provided little more than a bed to sleep in and a roof over their heads. There were other structures in the camp to deliver essential services to the operation. Among them were typically a blacksmith shop, tool shed, administration offices, a mess hall and a latrine.

The men housed at Camp Mac were responsible for some of the more notable features in Cheaha State Park. In conjunction with the National Park System, the CCC built Cheaha Lake and its stone bathhouse, eleven stone cabins, two stone pavilions, the Bunker Tower and the Bald Rock Group Lodge. Another of its achievements that's off the beaten path is Horn Mountain tower. It was built by the CCC as a fire lookout tower and is located on FS-200, a road that many people refer to as the Old CCC Road. Of course, the road was built by the CCC too. The dirt road isn't particularly well maintained, so a four-wheel-drive vehicle is recommended, but if you make it to the fire tower, you'll be greeted with a stunning view of the landscape below and be in the company of a historical monument built by the men of the CCC. A pavilion has been added and makes for a quiet picnic spot.

In 1948, the former superintendent of Talladega County schools, Mr. E.A. McBride, purchased the old CCC camp and founded Camp Mac, which was named in his honor by the first group of campers. McBride formed the camp on the principle that the classroom is not the only thing that children need to grow into successful, productive adults. Since Camp Mac was formed, the story of Mr. Taylor's eyes has been told around the campfires. On a fateful night in the very neighborhood where Camp Mac now stands, Mr. Taylor and three other men were gambling and enthusiastically partaking in the consumption of alcohol. As the evening wore on, one of the men excused himself to go down to the spring for a drink of water. While he was gone, Mr. Taylor and the two other men got into a drunken brawl. In the heat of passion that drunken brawls sometimes cause, Mr. Taylor was killed and his head severed from his body. It rolled across the floor, and upon reaching its stopping point, Mr. Taylor's eyes were firmly affixed to the men who had done him in.

Frightened out of their drunkenness, the two men began planning how they would escape the consequences of their actions. Since the first man was taking his time at the spring, and counting on the fact that he would surely still be near a drunken stupor when he returned, they decided they would convince him that the whole incident was of his doing. Upon his return, the plan was executed to success. The scapegoat was so befuddled in his state that he was unable to contradict his accusers. He was convicted of the crime and served several years in prison.

Many years later, after the scapegoat was released from prison, he returned to the scene of the crime. There, he heard a voice calling to him. Looking around, he saw the head of Mr. Taylor, his eyes fixed firmly on him. Mr. Taylor began to speak, but the man was so terrified that he didn't wait to see what Mr. Taylor had to say. Instead, he fled the area as quickly as any other man in his situation would. The residual story is that people walking in the woods today are apt to see the eyes of Mr. Taylor staring at them and begging them to come back so that he can tell them who really killed him.

Admittedly, this sounds like any old campfire story made up to scare children and has no basis in fact, but the legend goes that one night at camp after this very story was told, one of the older boys stood up and said, "There's no way that story is real." He was contradicted by one of the younger in the group, who said, "I know the story is true. Mr. Taylor was my uncle." Is the story real? There's no way to know for sure. We'll just have to leave that up to you, the reader, to decide.

CURRY STATION ROAD

Curry Station Road is located in Munford and was once known as Greensport Road. Greensport is a town no longer and lies under the waters of Neely Henry Dam. For a time though, Greensport was a very important piece of real estate. Boasting the first steamboat in Alabama, it became a nucleus of commercial traffic for northern Alabama. In addition to its financial impacts on Alabama, Curry Station Road and the town of Greensport have a history of Civil War skirmishes and wicked slave owners that won't soon let its history die.

Curry Station itself is a former railroad station, as well as the former homestead of the Curry family. It is nestled in the community of Kelly's Springs. Kelly's Springs got its name because it was once a reservation belonging to James Kelly, a leader of the Creek tribe of Indians, and because several large springs originate here and combine to form Kelly's Creek. Kelly's Springs was sold in 1832—the same year Talladega became a county—to Elijah Walker for the amount of $2,000. That was a tidy sum in those days.

Colonel William Curry, who was a veteran of the War of 1812, bought the land from Walker in 1837. The year after, Colonel Curry moved his family from Lincoln County, Georgia, to Talladega County. He built a grand estate and became a successful planter. He rose to be one of the richest men in the county and was credited with bringing the first railroad to the area. The home and other plantation structures he built are not standing today, but they were seen by the playwright Augustin Thomas and are the setting for his play *Alabama*.

On July 4, 1845, the appropriately named steamboat *Coosa* was launched. It was built in Cincinnati, Ohio, and traveled down the Ohio and Mississippi Rivers to New Orleans. From there, it traveled across the Mississippi Sound to Mobile, where it entered the Alabama River systems. Wetumpka is the highest point north of the Coosa River that is navigable by ship because of a nasty set of rapids named the Devil's Staircase. Once the steamboat *Coosa* arrived there, it had to stop and be disassembled and carried the rest of the way to Greensport by oxen-driven wagons. In Greensport, it was reassembled and commissioned. Thousands of people gathered from afar to witness the launching of the *Coosa*. A free barbecue was organized, and the people celebrated Independence Day and the "splashing" of the *Coosa* in tandem. Almost immediately, the *Coosa* gained a contract to haul mail from Greensport to Rome, Georgia, and soon after, it began hauling goods of all sorts. Greensport was now on the map.

As an aside, the creator of *Popeye the Sailorman*, Tom Sims, lived near the area and worked in shipping on the Coosa River. Popeye and other characters invented by Sims were all based on real people he knew growing up and working on his father's boat, the *Leota*. In fact, he once said, "When I began writing the script for *Popeye* I put my characters back on the old *Leota* that I knew as a boy, transformed it into a ship and made the Coosa River a salty sea."

The Civil War came, and the Curry residence was soon transformed into Camp Curry. When recruiters enlisted men, they were sent to Camp Curry as well as several other similar camps around the country for training. The enlistees at Camp Curry were known to march on the front lawn of the Curry Plantation, which has been noted as being a majestic sight. Later in the war, when the Union forces marched through Talladega, they crossed the Coosa River at Greensport. Upon arriving, they found the ferry docked to the opposite riverbank. That proved to be little deterrent for the Union forces though. They sent men to retrieve the ferry and bring it to the other side.

The ferry itself was small and would take far too long to transport all the Union forces across the river. However, it was needed to transport ambulances and other larger supply wagons. A small detachment of cavalry men was left behind to safeguard the river-crossing operation, and the others went to Ten Islands to ford the river there. Having gotten wind of what was happening, Brigadier General James Holt Clanton was determined to stop the Union forces from crossing the Coosa with his small band of two hundred Rebel cavalry. General Clanton's forces met the Union cavalry at the crossings of both Ten Islands and at Greensport. Being outnumbered by more than six to one, he managed to do little more than become a nuisance. The Union cavalry successfully crossed the Coosa, losing very few men, but General Clanton continued to wage his guerrilla warfare. General Rousseau, the commander of the Union troops, sent Clanton a message stating that if Clanton continued to follow him, he would "turn and thrash him soundly." Clanton withdrew and went to Wilsonville to enforce the railroad located there. The railroad at Curry Station was consequently struck, and Rousseau's men marched virtually unimpeded into Talladega.

Located not far up the road from where the Curry Plantation once stood was another plantation known as Jemison Place. Andrew Jackson's men stopped to rest here when they were on their way to the Battle of Talladega. Supposedly, the owner of the house would punish his slaves by shackling them in heavy irons in a small building behind the house. The slaves feared and hated this practice so much that upon their deaths, they still rattle their chains so loudly that they can be heard inside the big house. When the Union troops moved through the area, some of them also stopped here. Supposedly, there was an altercation in the kitchen of the plantation house, and a man was shot. He fell, and his blood covered the floor, creating a large stain. Even after hundreds of scrubbings, the bloodstain could never be removed.

A more recent account from the haunted Curry Station Road comes to us from John Wood. The first encounter that John had was when he was home for Christmas holidays as a teenager in 1993. He was with two friends in a car heading to a friend's farm. It was somewhat late, and they suddenly hit a patch of dense fog and could barely see. The fog lifted at the bridge crossing the Cheaha Creek, and there, in the headlights, was a faceless creature that threw its arm up over its nonexistent eyes when the headlights hit it. It was a very bizarre sight. The driver of the car swerved to miss it, but the ghostly person never moved or tried to get out of the way. They all saw it and lost their wits. It felt very evil and dark. John's heart was still pounding when he arrived home, and he had trouble falling asleep that night, fearful of what he had just seen. The best way John can describe what he saw was that it was a large-statured person, possibly female, who was wearing a cloak of fabric over its entire body except for where the face should have been.

Two years later, John was again with his friends going out to the farm to visit. This time, they encountered a woman walking in the road. She appeared to be holding something that resembled a baby. Her back was to them, and she was clad in a long, loose-fitting white dress, which was odd to them and caused them to take notice. Her head was draped with white fabric as well. Her walk was very methodical. The driver swerved to miss her, but they thought they might have hit her, so they turned around to check. The woman was now on the other side of the road walking with her back toward them again. They turned around once more to see if they could catch a glimpse of her face or what she was holding, and this time she had vanished. Where she was in the road, there was only a steep embankment on either side, so it didn't make sense that she went into the deep ditch to hide. He didn't feel that this woman was evil like the first encounter he had with the faceless being. Instead, he felt that they were probably bothering it more than anything. Studying photos of midwives from the 1800s, this woman's dress and head covering sound very similar to what they would have worn back in the day. Where this ghostly midwife was going with a newborn baby in the middle of the night is quite a mystery. Perhaps she was heading to the bridge to throw an unwanted baby over the side in the cover of darkness as was sometimes done back then, as horrible as it seems.

Several known atrocities are associated with Curry Station Road, and there are probably hundreds more that have been undocumented or left untold, such as the case of the mysterious woman in white. Between the war that passed through and the malevolent slave owner who once lived here, there really is no way to know all the barbarities that happened here. However, just like the bloodstain on the floor of Jemison Place, some evil deeds can never be washed away.

BIBLIOGRAPHY

BOOKS

Blackford, Randolph F. *Fascinating Talladega County*. Talladega, AL: Brannon Printing Company, 1957.

Crider, Beverly. *Legends and Lore of Birmingham and Central Alabama*. Charleston, SC: The History Press, 2014.

East, Don C. A Historical Analysis of the Creek Indian Hillabee Towns. Bloomington, IN: iUniverse, 2008.

Ellisor, John T. The Second Creek War: Interethnic Conflict and Collusion on a Collapsing Frontier. Lincoln: University of Nebraska Press, 2010.

Evans, David. Sherman's Horsemen: Union Cavalry Operations in the Atlanta Campaign. Bloomington: Indiana University Press, 1996.

The Heritage of Talladega County, Alabama. Clanton, AL: Heritage Publishing Consultants, Inc., n.d.

Hughes, John S. "Introduction." *An Insight into an Insane Asylum*. Tuscaloosa: University of Alabama, 2010.

Jemison, E. Grace. *Historic Tales of Talladega*. Talladega, AL: Talladega Press, 2010.

Owen, Thomas M., and Marie Bankhead Owen. *History of Alabama and Dictionary of Alabama Biography*. Vol. 4. Chicago: S.J. Clarke, 1921.

Sims, Louise M. *The Last Chief of the Kewahatchie*. Raleigh, NC: Pentland Press, Inc., 1997.

Stiggins, George, and William Stokes Wyman. *Creek Indian History: A Historical Narrative of the Genealogy, Traditions, and Downfall of the Ispocoga or Creek Indian Tribe of Indians*. Tuscaloosa: University of Alabama, 1989.

Sulzby, James F. *Historic Alabama Hotels and Resorts*. Tuscaloosa: University of Alabama, 1960.

ARTICLES

Anniston Star. "Big New Industry Going to Munford." January 9, 1944, 1.

———. "Munford Plant Hit by Blaze." August 8, 1950, 1.

———. "New Munford Foundry Opens." May 7, 1944, 5.

———. "Owner of Munford Foundry Meets Local Industrialists." January 14, 1944, 1.

Atlanta Constitution. "A Lady Outraged in Chilton County—Crime at Childersburg." May 9, 1885, 4.

Baldwin, B.J. "History of Child Labor Reform in Alabama." *Annals of the American Academy of Political and Social Science* 38 (July 1911): 111–13.

Bolton, Michael C. "Off-Road Vehicle Park in Talladega County Becomes Economic Boon." AL.com. July 29, 2012.

Campbell, Charles F., ed. "Joseph Henry Johnson." *Outlook for the Blind* 8 (1913): 94–95.

Daily Democrat [Huntington, IN]. "The Rope." May 17, 1892, 1.

Daily Home. "Open the Doors for April in Talladega." April 4, 2014.

Demmons, Doug. "Creek Medicine Man Lifts 'Curse' from Talladega Superspeedway." AL.com. *Birmingham News*, October 22, 2009.

Hall, Cody. "Negro Ex-Convict Faces Charges in Man's Death." *Anniston Star*, November 17, 1954, 1.

Harris, Daron. "Chinnabee Gravesite Holds Secrets of Its Own." *Daily Home*, July 25, 2014.

Hinton, Ed. "They're Hearing Voices at Talladega." ESPN.com, April 23, 2009.

Jasper, Paul. "The Ironaton, Alabama Pit." *Meteoritics* 2, no. 2 (1964): 175–76.

Layton, Fred L. "Kymulga Cave." *Journal of Spelean History* 28, no. 1 (January–February 1994): 1–3.

McGee, Ryan. "Strange Things Happen When Cup Drivers Try to Tame Talladega." ESPN.com, April 4, 2008.

Reeves, Jay. "Childersburg: A Quiet Town with a Past of Gambling, Bootlegging." *Tuscaloosa News*, January 23, 1995, 4.

Robertson, Blair. "Group Restoring Old Mill." *Montgomery Advertiser*, April 21, 1991.

Scott, Vern, ed. "The Lawrence O'Donovan Home." *Talladega County Historical Association Newsletter* 10 (Aug. 1973): 20-22. Print.

Times Daily [Florence, AL]. "Munford Shooting Suspect Arrested." November 4, 2005, 2.

Vandiver, Wellington. "Pioneer Talladega, Its Minutes and Memories." *Alabama Historical Quarterly* 2, no. 16 (Summer 1954): 218–19.

Weiss, Kenneth R. "Few Military Bases in South to Be Cut." *Wilmington Morning Star*, December 30, 1988, 1.

"Women Rapidly Enroll in Wet Organizations." *St. Petersburg Times*, September 16, 1931, 1.

UNPUBLISHED SOURCES

Haveman, Christopher D. "The Removal of the Creek Indians from the Southeast, 1825–1838." PhD dissertation, Auburn University, 2009.

Perry, Robert E., and Carey B. Oakley. *Letter Report of Investigations at Fort Williams Memorial*. Rep. no. 6187-06-1305. Sylacauga, AL: MACTEC, 2006.

Pursell Farms & Resort. *The Old Hamilton Place*. Sylacauga, AL: Pursell Farms & Resort, 2013.

INTERVIEWS

Adams, Adrienne. March 28, 2015, Top Trails.

Atkisson, Billy. December 30, 2014, Talladega County and Courthouse.

Barnett, Jim. April 3, 2015, Cemetery Mountain.

Bryant, Jessica Atkisson. February 20, 2015, Gloria's bridge.

Caine, Randy. April 30, 2015, Buttermilk Hill.

Davis, Becky. March 9, 2015, Town's End Farm.

Foster, Danny. January 8, 2013, Talladega County Legends.

Francis, Thomas. September 5, 2014, Kymulga Grist Mill and Bridge.

Green, Mark, and Shirley Green. September 5, 2014, Kymulga Grist Mill and Bridge.

Hanner, Lynne. April 11, 2014, AIDB.

Hill, Patty, and Terry Hill. April 12, 2014, Swan Hall.

Kirk, Erin. August 26, 2014, McElderry Plantation.

Lavender, Judith. February 23, 2015, Talladega County.

Lynch, Michael. April 19, 2015, AIDB.

Manget, Crystal Massey. January 2, 2015, Cofield House.

McClendon, Algalene. February 19, 2015, Buttermilk Hill.

McClendon, Kara. April 30, 2015, Buttermilk Hill.

Reeves, Michael. August 26, 2014, McElderry Plantation.

———. February 22, 2015, Fort Williams Memorial.

Shropshire, Jennifer. March 3, 2015, Munford Foundry.

Sorenson, Jarred, and Joy Sorenson. April 18, 2015, Desoto Caverns.

Tipton, Stephanie. April 26, 2015, Buttermilk Hill.

Waldrop, Michael. April 30, 2015, Buttermilk Hill.

WEBSITES

Abandoned & Little-Known Airfields. www.airfields-freeman.com.

Alabama Institute for Deaf and Blind. aidb.org.

Alabama Pioneers. alabamapioneers.com.

Alabama Trails, War of 1812. www.alabamatrailswar1812.com.

Alabama Women's Hall of Fame. www.awhf.org.

CASPIR Paranormal Team. www.caspirparanormal.com

Encyclopedia.com. www.encyclopedia.com.

Encyclopedia of Alabama. www.encyclopediaofalabama.org.

ESPN. sports.espn.go.com.

ExploreSouthernHistory.com. www.exploresouthernhistory.com.

Family Search. familysearch.org.

Find a Grave. www.findagrave.com.

Flickr. www.flickr.com.

Free Travel with Us. freetravelwithus.com.

Haunted Talladega County. www.facebook.com/hauntedtalladega.

IMDB. www.imdb.com.

JSTOR. www.jstor.org.

Justia US Law. law.justia.com.

Military Wikia. military.wikia.com.

Mosaic Templars Cultural Center. www.mosaictemplarscenter.com.

OldHouses.com. www.oldhouses.com.

Oxford Paranormal Society. oxfordparanormalsociety.com.

Pursell Farms. pursellfarms.com.

Rivers of Alabama. www.riversofalabama.org.

Rootsweb. www.rootsweb.ancestry.com.

Treasure Net. treasurenet.com.

University of Alabama Press. www.uapress.ua.edu.

U.S. Army Center of Military History. history.army.mil.

USGenWeb Archives. files.usgwarchives.net.

Waymarking.com. www.waymarking.com.

Wikipedia. en.wikipedia.org.

World History Project. worldhistoryproject.org.

ABOUT THE AUTHORS

Courtesy of Kat Hobson.

When not leading her team of paranormal investigators into dark, spooky places throughout the Southeast, Kim Johnston can be found spending time with her family in her Vestavia, Alabama home. She is the mother of three children and the devoted wife to the love of her life, Dan. She graduated from Auburn University at Montgomery and holds a degree in psychology. Kim works full time as a software developer in the banking industry. She is the founder of Spirit Communications and Research (S.C.A.Re) and has been investigating paranormal phenomena since 2011 after events in her own home made her curious. Her team has investigated grand old places such as the Thomas Jefferson Hotel in downtown Birmingham and has even spent the night locked inside the brick walls of Fort Morgan. Her team also does private home investigations and has helped many local families cope with hauntings. She can be contacted at Kim@scareofal.com. For more information about her team, please visit www.scareofal.com.

Shane Busby was born and raised in Talladega County, where he spent most of his summers working on his grandfather's farm in rural Alpine. Today, Shane works full time as a software engineer and is a graduate of the University of Alabama in Birmingham. In his free time, he enjoys sailing, metal working and electronics. Shane's journey into investigating the things that go bump in the night started early. As a child, he read every piece of literature he could find concerning the paranormal. As an adult, Shane is every bit as voracious about figuring out the secrets of the universe as he has ever been. When night falls, you just might find him out exploring one of those places that most people dare not go with the paranormal investigation team that he co-founded, Spirit Communications and Research (S.C.A.Re). Shane can be contacted at Shane@scareofal.com.